THE EMPIRE
OF THE
HOLY SPIRIT

THE EMPIRE OF THE HOLY SPIRIT

Reflections on biblical and historical patterns of life in the Spirit

MICHAEL A.G. HAYKIN

Published by: H&E Academic, Peterborough, Canada
www.hesedandemet.com

Cover design by Chance Faulkner
Cover image: Pentecost, the Holy Spirit descends upon the apostles—Psalter of Eleanor of Aquitaine (*c.*1185)

Third Edition, 2020, H&E Publishing
Paperback ISBN: 978-1-989174-71-5
Hardcover ISBN: 978-1-989174-73-9
eBook ISBN: 978-1-989174-72-2

"Michael Haykin's *The Empire of the Holy Spirit* is not just a book about the Holy Spirit. This is a book written, obviously, by one who knows the Person (not just the topic) of which he writes. This book will prompt you to think. You'll want to scratch down notes, and talk about insights over coffee with friends. But, more than that, this book will prompt you to get on your knees, through the Spirit of God, and cry out 'Abba Father!'"
—**Russell D. Moore**, President, The Ethics & Religious Liberty Commission

"Besides Michael Haykin, few people, to my knowledge, could have written such a book as this with the same credibility. The richness of the combination of history, theology, spirituality, and practicality in this volume could come only from someone who has the expertise of a professor of church history and spirituality, the insight of a biblical scholar, the wisdom of an experienced church elder, and the authenticity of a sincere personal piety."
—**Donald S. Whitney**, Senior Associate Dean, The Southern Baptist Theological Seminary

"Those familiar with the work of Michael Haykin will know it is always orthodox, pastoral, insightful, and practical. In this volume it is very much business as usual, and the reader will not be disappointed. In a series of connected essay, Dr. Haykin explores the person and work of the Holy Spirit in a manner which honours scripture, draws helpfully on church tradition, and applies the findings to the everyday of the contemporary church. Highly recommended."
—**Carl Trueman**, Professor of Biblical and Religious Studies, Grove City College, PA

"Michael Haykin combines his outstanding historical, theological and biblical scholarship with a warm-hearted spirituality in this stimulating work on the vital subject of the Holy Spirit."
—**Robert Strivens**, Pastor, Bradford-on-Avon Baptist Church, Wiltshire

"Haykin's *Empire of the Spirit* covers a rich cluster of subjects on the Holy Spirit from various biblical, historical, and theological perspectives. Whether speaking about the Spirit's role in sanctification, in revival, in the Great Commission, in the exercise of genuine success, or in promoting Christian unity, Haykin's thoughts, tethered to Scripture, offer an exciting read. This book needs to be pondered over and yet is a page-turner. I pray that it may promote a deepening interest in and appreciation for the Spirit's indispensable, variegated ministry in the lives of believers."

—**Joel R. Beeke**, President, Puritan Reformed Theology Seminary, Grand Rapids, MI

"In *The Empire of the Holy Spirit* Dr. Haykin is simply at his finest. He pursues the thesis that the invisible kingdom of the Spirit is present throughout history and Christians live under its all-encompassing reign.

Armed with the prodigious skills of a historical and biblical theologian, the author combines the best of Patristic and Puritan thinking upon several aspects of the Spirit's work with first-rate exegesis of relevant New Testament texts. The upshot is that he successfully navigates the discourse on the Spirit and his work further away from the contemporary rut in which it has languished.

More importantly, he has gifted the Church with a lucid, insightful, and compelling treatment on a vital subject. Like a draught of fresh, cold water on a hot and muggy day, this work will reinvigorate and spur you to live under the aegis of the Holy Spirit."

—**Glendon G. Thompson**, President, Toronto Baptist Seminary and Bible College; Senior Pastor of Jarvis Street Baptist Church, Toronto, CA

"This work is Michael Haykin at his best. It reflects years of reflection on the person and work of the Holy Spirit—a topic which desperately needs more attention today—and it is a rare combination of biblical, theological, and historical work. In a short space, this work introduces us to the entire range of historical theology on key aspects of the Spirit's work. It traverses Patristic thought, Reformation thinking, as well as the mature reflections of the Puritans and early Calvinistic Baptists. It demonstrates well how the church throughout the ages, rooted in Scripture, rightly views the Spirit as the sanctifier of the elect, the co-fulfiller of the Great Commission, the creator of Christian unity and love, the agent of true prayer and genuine revival. It also provides a helpful chapter on discerning true spirituality in a postmodern age. This work is must reading if you want to learn more about the precious work of the Spirit of God. May we learn its lessons and see once again in our day a mighty revival of God's Spirit upon his people for our good and the glory of the Gospel."

—**Stephen J. Wellum**, Professor of Christian Theology,
The Southern Baptist Theological Seminary

"A gifted historian and solid theologian, Michael Haykin has gained a well-deserved reputation as a leading authority on the Church Fathers. In The Empire of the Holy Spirit, this Patristic scholar has given us a priceless treasure that combines seasoned intellect with a passion for true spirituality. Haykin masterfully weaves together the historical theology of the early church leaders with pastoral piety in presenting this engaging study of the person and work of the Holy Spirit. The result is both profound and persuasive. This book will surely challenge all who read it to walk in complete dependence upon the sovereign power of the Spirit."

—**Steven J. Lawson**, President and Founder of OnePassion Ministries

"In this inspiring and delightful study, the much loved historian of the Spirit, Michael Haykin, brings both his vast scholarship and genuine piety to bear on this routinely neglected doctrine. Michael has a masterful touch that combines devotional warmth and keen depth of insight. The fruit of decades of reflection and experience, "The Empire of the Spirit" will not only inform but minister life to those that read it. Reaching back for wisdom, it points us forward in hope, as the Spirit extends the empire of Christ throughout the ages through his faithful elect. I should not be surprised if this book becomes a modern spiritual classic in the evangelical tradition."

—**Joe Boot**, Founder of Ezra Institute for Contemporary Christianity; Senior Pastor of Westminster Chapel, Toronto, ON

"For as long as I have known Michael Haykin, he has cared deeply about the work of the Spirit in the church. The close connection between the Spirit's activity and the church that Christ died for is often missing in many modern writings on the Spirit. For many modern writers the work of the Spirit is conceived of as purely an individual experience. In this edifying book, Michael marries the work of the Spirit solidly to the cross and to the church that was gifted to Christ because of his cross-work. This book calls churches back to being 'people of the Spirit' in our preaching, praying, living and loving."

—**Tim Kerr**, Dean of Students, Toronto Baptist Seminary

"Jesus' words in Matthew 13:52 certainly apply to Michael Haykin. Michael is a grammateus—a man of learning—and more importantly, he is mathēteutheis—'discipled'—in what relates to God's Kingdom. His book presents to us, out of the storeroom of his scholarship and his experience of God, 'new treasures as well as old'. Michael has written a rich and stimulating study which emphasizes the importance of pneumatology (often a Cinderella subject) in Scripture, in Patristic literature, and in many Christian teachers up to modern times. He writes not as a detached observer but as one who has long experienced the Spirit's transforming power in his own life. He presents his subject, not as a matter of academic interest, but as one of vital importance for everyone who desires to know and serve God 'in the Spirit'. Reading this book has been both a challenge and a blessing!"

—**The late Maurice Dowling**, Professor of Church History, Irish Baptist College; Constituent College of Queen's University, Belfast, N. Ireland

To the memory of my beloved mother,
Teresa Veronica Haykin,
who went to be with the Lord on March 9, 1976—
"Precious in the sight of the Lord
is the death of his saints."

(Psalm 116:15)

I shall open my mouth,
And His Spirit will speak through me
the glorious praise of the Lord and his beauty…

Ode of Solomon 16.6[1]
(*c*.120)

---

[1] Trans. James H. Charlesworth, *The Earliest Christian Hymnbook: The Odes of Solomon* (Eugene: Cascade Books, 2009), 45.

Contents

INTRODUCTION

All Christian character is royal.
The most insignificant stone in this spiritual temple is sublime. The imperial agencies of the
Holy Spirit give grandeur to the poorest lives. There is not one so low and ignorant but that
brought beneath the regenerating and purifying influences of God's saving grace shall one day
shine in burnished beauty.

B.D. Thomas
(1843–1917)

My interest in the person and the work of the Holy Spirit began
not long after my conversion. I can testify to the glory of God that
it was the Spirit of Christ that led me to the Saviour during the fall
of 1973 and the winter of 1974. On Friday, February 22, of 1974,
the day following my conscious surrender to the Lordship of Jesus, I was returning by bus from Toronto to Hamilton, Ontario,
where I worked on weekends. I had an unforgettable sense of the
presence of the Spirit: as Jesus promised his disciples, in the new
covenant his Spirit of truth would be in them (John 14:26). My
interest in the Spirit's work subsequently ran along two channels:
my study of patristic pneumatology in my M.Rel. and Th.D., from
1974–1982,[1] and my involvement in the Charismatic movement
between 1974 and 1979 or so. While I came to reject much of what
passed for biblical Christianity in the Charismatic movement, I
never lost my interest in pneumatology. My embrace of Calvinistic Baptist convictions in the early 1980s did nothing to lessen this
interest, for I discovered the profound fascination the Puritans

---

[1] The fruit of this was my thesis, which has been published as *The Spirit of God: The
Exegesis of 1 and 2 Corinthians in the Pneumatomachian Controversy of the Fourth Century*
(Leiden: E.J. Brill, 1994).

1

had with regard to pneumatology as well as the eighteenth-century origins of the Evangelical movement in some of the greatest displays of the Spirit's power in the history of the Church. And those men and women of the English Baptist community at the close of the eighteenth century with whom I increasingly identified in thought, ethos, and piety, were deeply conscious of the importance of the Spirit in their lives and sought to cultivate what Richard Lovelace has called "a theology of radical dependence on the Spirit."[2] As one of them, John Sutcliff (1752–1814) of Olney, once remarked:

> The outpouring of the divine Spirit ... is the grand promise of the New Testament ... His influences are the soul, the great animating soul of all religion. These withheld, divine ordinances are empty cisterns, and spiritual graces are withering flowers. These suspended, the greatest human abilities labour in vain, and the noblest efforts fail of success.[3]

In more recent days, as I have been teaching a significant number of courses on the Ancient Church and on biblical spirituality as the central part of my responsibilities at The Southern Baptist Theological Seminary, I have been struck afresh by the importance of classical pneumatological thought for the post-

---

[2] "Pneumatological Issues in American Presbyterianism," *Greek Orthodox Theological Review* 31 (1986): 345–346.

[3] *Jealousy for the Lord of Hosts illustrated* (London: W. Button, 1791), 12. See also *The Authority and Sanctification of the Lord's Day, Explained and Enforced* (n.p., 1786), 8: "Be earnest with God for the gift of his *Holy Spirit*, in an abundant measure. Seek his divine influences, to furnish you with *spiritual* ability, in order that you may be found in the discharge of that which is your indispensible duty. Highly prize his sacred operations. These are the real excellency of all religious duties. Brilliant parts and abilities, natural or acquired, can never supply their place." The fruit of my reading the eighteenth-century Calvinistic Baptists was *One heart and one soul: John Sutcliff of Olney, his friends, and his times* (Darlington, Co. Durham: Evangelical Press, 1994), which was a real joy to research and write. A second edition is forthcoming from H&E Publishing.

Reformation people of God as well as by the way in which Puritan and early Calvinistic Baptist teaching about the Spirit forms a fitting complement to Patristic thought. It needs noting that the best representatives of both of these traditions were certain that to seek the Spirit's strength apart from various appointed means in the church was both unbiblical and utterly foolish. The most important theologian in the second century, Irenaeus of Lyons (*c.*130–*c.*200), thus rightly stated about those who refuse to join themselves to other believers:

> Those who do not join themselves to the Church do not share in him [i.e. the Spirit]. … Where the Church is, there is the Spirit of God; where the Spirit of God is, there is the Church and every grace. The Spirit is truth. Therefore those who do not share in the Spirit are neither nourished to life from the mother's breast nor do they enjoy that most clear fountain which springs from the body of Christ.[4]

This same conviction lies behind Cyprian's famous statement that "outside of the church there is no salvation,"[5] which is picked up by *The Westminster Confession of Faith* when it states that "out of" the universal church "there is no ordinary possibility of salvation."[6] Benjamin Keach (1640–1704), the most significant Calvinistic Baptist theologian of the late seventeenth century, essentially makes the same point in 1681. In a direct allusion to the Quakers, who dispensed with the sacraments of baptism and the Lord's Supper, Keach said,

---

[4] *Against Heresies* 3.24.1, trans. J. Patout Burns and Gerald M. Fagin, *The Holy Spirit* (Message of the Fathers of the Church, vol. 3; Wilmington, Delaware: Michael Glazier, Inc., 1984), 36.

[5] *Letter* 72.21.

[6] *The Westminster Confession of Faith* 25.2. It is noteworthy that *The Second London Confession* omits this statement.

> Many are confident they have the Spirit, Light, and Power, when 'tis all mere delusion. ... Some men boast of the Spirit, and conclude they have the Spirit, and none but they, and yet at the same time cry down and vilify his blessed ordinances and Institutions, which he hath left in his Word, carefully to be observed and kept, till he comes the second time without sin unto salvation. ...The Spirit hath its proper bounds, and always runs in its spiritual channel, *viz*. the Word and ordinances, God's public and private worship.[7]

This book then is the fruit of an interface in my mind and heart of ancient pneumatological perspectives with more modern ones as I seek to explore what the Scriptures have to say about living under the rule of the Holy Spirit. World history is taken up with the rise and fall of earthly empires. The century just past witnessed the fall of a number—one thinks of the British and Dutch Empires—as well as the rapid rise and collapse of others—the "Thousand-year" Reich in Germany, for instance, or the Soviet Empire. But there is another history—that wrought by the Spirit of God—in which the Spirit is building the kingdom of the Lord Jesus. And it is of this alternative Empire that this book speaks. After a chapter in which the personhood and deity of the Holy Spirit is outlined, the book looks at various elements of the Spirit's work as the Father's gift to believers, as the Sanctifier of the elect of God, as the co-Fulfiller of the Great Commission, as the Promoter of Christian unity, as the Agent of true prayer and genuine revival, as the Source of all true Christian success, as the Creator of real love, and as the Dethroner of spiritual idols of the

---

[7] *Tropologia: A Key to Open Scripture-Metaphors* (London: Enoch Prosser, 1681), II, 312, 314, modernized.

contemporary culture. In all of this, we are tracing the historical patterns of the imperial work of the Spirit.

A number of the book's chapters (Chapters 4, 7 and 8) arose in connection with a trip I took to England and Wales in June of 2008 to speak at the Evangelical Movement of Wales Ministers' Conference, held in beautiful Bala, Wales, from June 16 to 18, 2008, and to give an address at the End of Year Service at London Theological Seminary, London, England, on June 14, 2008. The hospitality afforded me by the seminary in London, especially by Philip Eveson and Robert Strivens, and by the ministers at the Bala conference was, and is, deeply appreciated. I am especially thankful to Pastor Graham Harrison, recently retired from forty-seven years of pastoral ministry at Emmanuel Church, Newport, Wales, and his dear wife, Eluned, for the many kindnesses they showed to myself and my daughter Victoria, who accompanied me on the trip.[8]

Much of the material in Chapter 3 began as a paper at "Our Holy God," a conference sponsored by the Alliance of Confessing Evangelicals, Nassau Christian Center, Princeton, on October 27, 2007, prior to its being used in an address at Bala. I am also indebted to my one-time research assistant, Mr. Allen R. Mickle, now senior pastor of Tunkhannock Baptist Church, Tunkhannock, Pennsylvania, for help with this chapter. The heart of chapters 2 and 5 go back to talks in the chapel of Central Baptist Seminary, Toronto, on January 19, 1984, and September 23, 1983, respectively. The section in Chapter 5 on the Puritans and prayer was originally part of an address at Audubon Drive Bible Church,

---

[8] For a booklet on his ministry, see *Rev. Graham Harrison: 47 Years of Ministry (1962–2010)* (Newport: Emmanuel Church, 2010). For an online version, see http://www.emmanuel-newport.org.uk/retirement.pdf.

Laurel, Mississippi, for their Reformation Day Conference, October 30, 1999.

I am very thankful to Pastor Jerry Marcellino for the privilege of speaking at this conference. It later appeared in Michael A.G. Haykin, ed., *Acorns to Oaks: The Primacy and Practice of Biblical Theology: A Festschrift for Dr. Geoff Adams* (Joshua Press, 2003) and is used here by permission. Chapter 6 first appeared in *Reformation Today* 115 (May–June 1990) and also appears here by permission. Chapter 9 was first given as a sermon in The Southern Baptist Theological Seminary Chapel, Thursday, October 30, 2008. I am deeply grateful to the invitation of Dr. R. Albert Mohler to preach on that occasion.

Chapter 1 is the substance of an address prepared for a series of studies on the Niceno-Constantinopolitan Creed held at St. George's Anglican Church (ANIC), Ottawa, during Lent, 2010. I am extremely thankful to my long-time friend the Rev. Dr. L. Gregory Bloomquist for this opportunity. The final chapters, Chapters 10 and 11, had their origins as a paper that was delivered at the Annual Meeting of the American Association of Christian Colleges and Seminaries, Inc., February 4, 2009, hosted by Detroit Baptist Theological Seminary. Drs. Jerry Priest, Mark Snoeberger and David Doran proved to be great hosts for the two days I was at this annual meeting.

It is over twenty years ago that I began to think of writing a book on the Holy Spirit. Initially I was going to base it on the teaching about the Holy Spirit in Paul's letter to the Ephesians, one of the richest sources of New Testament pneumatology. This is not that book. Of the chapters of that book, only one has substantially survived over the years to be included in this small volume (Chapter 2). In some ways, I am very glad that that projected volume never saw the light of day. Understandably the chapters in this volume are not all that I would like to say about the Spirit. There is nothing about the gifts of the Holy Spirit, the *charismata*, about which I thought and spoke much in the 1970s and 1980s. Nor is there anything about the witness of the Spirit in the early Christian martyrs, beginning with Stephen. Maybe chapters on those will appear in a subsequent book. What is here, though, captures much of what I regard to be central to Christian thought about the Spirit. May the One of whom these chapters speak use them for the glory of Christ.

Michael A.G. Haykin
Dundas, Ontario
March 9, 2010

A note on the second edition
I wish to thank Dr. Roger Duke and Brian Mooney for working with me on the publication of the first edition of this book. Their encouragement and help were wonderful.

Apart from stylistic changes in the typesetting, the correction of one or two errors, and the insertion of a few sentences in Chapter 11, the only major difference between this second edition and the first one is the inclusion of chapter 9 on Charles Haddon Spurgeon's pneumatology. This new chapter serves to illustrate the theme of the previous chapter that deals with Paul's reflections on the power of the Spirit in 2 Timothy 1. This chapter on Spurgeon was originally given as a lecture at Toronto Baptist Seminary on January 30, 1992, the centennial of the death of Spurgeon. I was deeply grateful to Dr. Geoff Adams, the Principal of the seminary at the time, for that invitation. Subsequent to the lecture, it appeared in print as "'Where the Spirit of God Is, There Is Power': An Introduction to Spurgeon's Teaching on the Holy

Spirit" in the *Churchman* 106 (1992): 197–208, and is used here by permission.

In drawing up the original lecture on Spurgeon, I was particularly struck by the nineteenth-century Baptist's quaint remark that the "the Holy Spirit always keeps sweet company with Jesus Christ." That to me seemed to go to the heart of New Testament pneumatology: the Spirit's great new covenant work is to glorify Christ, to draw men and women to this glorious Savior, to cause them to live for him and find their deepest joys in him. If this keynote of New Testament pneumatology (see, for example, John 16:13–14 in this regard) is absent, we are not in step with the Spirit of Jesus whatever else we might say about the Spirit.

Dundas, Ontario
May 26, 2016

A note on the third edition

I wish to thank Chance Faulkner and Corey Hughes of H&E Publishing for this great opportunity to reprint this work under the auspices of their publishing house.

I realize that I need to say a word about the title, specifically, why I have chosen to use the word "empire." For many, this term has negative associations—imperialism is regarded in the modern world with both disdain and disgust. My use of the term "empire of the Holy Spirit" is along the lines laid down by Augustine in his classic work, *On the City of God*, in which history is ultimately to be understood as the struggle between two cities, that of God and that of men. And eventually the City of God will be victorious in this struggle. "The empire of the Holy Spirit" thus bespeaks that triumphant realm belonging to the Holy Spirit in which he is active in power and love, turning the affections of sinners to Christ and to God his Father. And unlike human empires that crush the spirit of men and women, this spiritual empire alone brings true freedom and genuine fulfillment.

Dundas, Ontario
August 1, 2020

1

WE BELIEVE IN THE HOLY SPIRIT

May none of God's wonderful works keep silence, night or morning.
Bright stars, high mountains, the depths of the seas,
sources of rushing rivers:
May all these break into song as we sing to Father, Son and Holy Spirit.

May all the angels in the heavens reply,
Amen! Amen! Amen!
Power, praise, honor, eternal glory to God, the only Giver of grace,
Amen! Amen! Amen![1]

Hymn
(Third century, found at Oxyrhynchus)

In his masterful study of the unfolding of early Christian thought, the late Jarolsav Pelikan (1923–2006) notes that the "climax of the doctrinal development of the early church was the dogma of the Trinity."[2] And the textual expression of that climax is undoubtedly the Niceno-Constantinopolitan Creed that was issued at the Council of Constantinople (381) to resolve once and for all the Arian crisis, which had dominated theological discussions throughout the fourth century. Through the teaching of Arius (260/280–336), an elder of the church at Alexandria in Egypt, the church in the Roman Empire was plunged into a lengthy, bitter controversy about the deity of Christ.[3] Arius claimed that only the Father was truly

---

[1] Cited Mark A. Noll, *Turning Points: Decisive Moments in the History of Christianity* (Grand Rapids: Baker Books, 1997), 47.

[2] *The Christian Tradition: Vol. 1: The Emergence of the Catholic Tradition (100–600)* (Chicago/London: The University of Chicago Press, 1971), 172.

[3] For studies of this controversy, see especially Pelikan, *Christian Tradition*, 1:172–225; R.P.C. Hanson, *The Search for the Christian Doctrine of God. The Arian Controversy 318–381* (1988 ed.; repr. Grand Rapids: Baker, 2005); John Behr, *The Formation of*

11

God. As he wrote in a letter to Alexander (d.328), the bishop of Alexandria, God the Father alone, "the cause of all, is without beginning." The Son was created by the Father as "an immutable and unchangeable perfect creature," and thus is "not everlasting or co-everlasting with the Father."[4] In Arius' words: "the Son has a beginning, but God is without beginning."[5] For Arius there was a time when the Son did not exist, a time when it is inappropriate to call God "Father." As for the Holy Spirit, by Arius' reckoning, he was even less divine than the Son, for he was the first of the creatures made by the Son.

A council called at Nicaea, near Constantinople, sought to resolve the situation with a creedal statement that unequivocally declared that the Lord Jesus Christ is "true God of true God, begotten not made, of one being (*homoousios*) with the Father." In other words, the Son is truly God in whatever sense the Father is God. The key phrase in this creed is undoubtedly the statement that the Son is "of one being (*homoousios*) with the Father." Here, the full deity of the Son is asserted, the term *homoousios* emphasising the fact that the Son shares the very being of Father. Whatever belongs to and characterises God the Father belongs to and characterises the Son. He is not a creature, contrary to the view of Arius and his fellow Arians. However, nothing was said in the original Nicene Creed about the Holy Spirit beyond the statement "[We believe] in the Holy Spirit."[6]

Christian Theology, Vol. 2: The Nicene Faith (Crestwood: St. Vladimir's Press, 2004), 2 vols. On Arius, see Behr, *The Nicene Faith*, 1:130–149. For a succinct statement of the philosophical and theological roots of Arianism, see Roldanus, *Church in the Age of Constantine*, 74–77.

[4] *Letter to Alexander of Alexandria*, trans. William G. Rusch, *The Trinitarian Controversy* (Philadelphia: Fortress Press, 1980), 31–32.

[5] Arius, *Letter to Eusebius of Nicomedia*, trans. Rusch, *Trinitarian Controversy*, 29–30.

[6] For a translation of the Nicene Creed, see J. N. D. Kelly, *Early Christian Creeds* (3rd ed.; Burnt Mill, Harlow, Essex: Longman Group Limited, 1972), 215–216.

In spite of what those who drafted this creed hoped, the Nicene Creed did not end the controversy begun by Arius' teaching. Eusebius of Nicomedia (died *c*.342), a worldly-wise ecclesiastical politician and supporter of Arius, had the ear of the professing Christian emperor, Constantine (*c*.272–337). Eusebius convinced Constantine that the condemnation of Arianism was far too harsh, and so various Arian leaders and even Arius were brought back into favour and leading enthusiasts for Nicaea and its creed sent packing. Among the latter was the great defender of Trinitarian orthodoxy in the fourth century, Athanasius of Alexandria (*c*.297–373).

Athanasius *contra mundum*

Alexander of Alexandria had died in 328, and was succeeded by Athanasius as bishop of Alexandria.[7] Probably a native Egyptian— he was mocked, for example, as "the black dwarf"—he was a theological genius. Until his death in 373 he was the most formidable opponent of Arianism in the Roman Empire. Yet, this defence was not without much personal suffering. No less than five times he was exiled from Alexandria, four of them definitely for his commitment to the theology of the Nicene Creed. One of his exiles was at the hands of the emperor Julian the Apostate (332–363), who disliked Athanasius simply because of the latter's commitment to Christianity.

Athanasius' theology is well seen in some letters that he wrote to a friend, Serapion of Thmuis (died after 362), in 358 and 359, while on the run from persecution by the Arian emperor Constantius II (317–361). From John 16:15—Jesus' statement that "all that belongs to the Father is mine"—and John 17:10—Jesus' words to the Father, "all you have is mine"—Athanasius reasons

---

[7] On the life and thought of Athanasius see especially Alvyn Petersen, *Athanasius* (Ridgefield/Harrisburg: Morehouse Publishing, 1995).

that the Son shares all of the divine attributes of the Father. "The Father is light," he writes, "the Son is radiance and true light. The Father is true God; the Son is true God."[8] John 16:15, Athanasius further notes, could never have been said by a creature, no matter how highly exalted a being. It is only appropriate from the mouth of one who is "one in being with the Father." Thus, Athanasius sums up: "of that which the Father has, there is nothing which does not belong to the Son." It is thus "impious" to say that "the Son is a creature."[9]

Arianism, Athanasius rightly saw, also imperilled the heart of the Christian gospel. Since salvation is of God, and God alone, then Christ, the mediator of that salvation, must be God. If Christ were a creature, as Arius claimed, then he could not save us, for a creature—no matter how perfect—cannot save another creature. The entire church owes this African Christian a great debt. His dogged determination to be faithful to his divine Lord led to the slogan *Athanasius contra mundum*, "Athanasius against the world." Athanasius refused to give way to political pressure and physical force from a succession of Arian emperors, for he rightly believed the faith of Nicaea to be that of the Scriptures.

The letters to Serapion also reveal that the divinity of the Holy Spirit was becoming a topic of theological conflict, for Serapion informed Athanasius that there were individuals in his community who were maintaining that the Holy Spirit is a creature, albeit of angelic nature.[10] In his response, Athanasius insisted that the Holy Spirit, as the Spirit of Christ, cannot be a creature. The belief that the Spirit is a creature blasphemes the Son since the Spirit is the Spirit *of Christ*. It also destroys the

---

[8] *Letter to Serapion* 2.2 (trans. C.R.B. Shapland, *The Letters of Saint Athanasius Concerning the Holy Spirit* [London: Epworth Press, 1951], 153).

[9] *Letter to Serapion* 2.2–3, 153–154.

[10] *Letter to Serapion* 1.1.

Christian concept of God, for it makes the Trinity consist of Creator and creature.[11] Athanasius' defence of the Spirit's divinity in the letters to Serapion appears to have helped him realize implicitly that the creedal formulation of Nicaea needed to be supplemented by a statement about the Spirit. Thus, at the Council of Alexandria, held in 362 and over which Athanasius presided, it was declared:

> [A]ll who desire peace with us [ought] … to anathematize the Arian heresy, to confess the faith that was confessed by the Holy Fathers at Nicaea, and also to anathematize those who say the Holy Spirit is a creature and separate him from the being of Christ. For a true departure from the loathsome heresy of the Arians is this: [a refusal] to divide the Holy Trinity, or to say that any member of it is a creature. For those who pretend to profess the faith confessed at Nicaea, but who dare to blaspheme against the Holy Spirit, do nothing more than deny the Arian heresy in words, while they hold it fast in thought.[12]

At the death of Athanasius in 373, the mantle of his struggle for a biblical understanding of the Trinity passed to the Cappadocian Basil of Caesarea (*c.*329–379), whom Athanasius once described as "the pride of the Church."[13]

---

[11] Michael A.G. Haykin, *The Spirit of God: The Exegesis of 1 and 2 Corinthians in the Pneumatomachian Controversy of the Fourth Century* (Leiden: E. J. Brill, 1994), 21.

[12] Athanasius, *Tome to the Antiochenes* 3, author's translation.

[13] Athanasius, *Letter to Palladius*, author's translation.

The Creed: a sign of Hellenization?

In many respects, Basil's main contribution to the history of dogma is his pneumatological thought.[14] Born into a long-standing Christian family—both sets of grandparents suffered during the brutal persecution of Diocletian (*c.*245–*c.*312)—Basil's conversion in 356 had come in the context of the early monastic movement that introduced him to an environment in which there was a distinct interest in the sanctifying work of the Holy Spirit. Basil's experience of the Spirit in the monastic life was definitely a key factor in a growing concern he had with the question of the nature and person of the Holy Spirit. This personal interest coincided with a rapid increase in the 360s and 370s of ontological questions about the being of the Spirit, of which Athanasius' dispute with certain individuals in Thmuis in the late 350s appears to have been a forerunner. Those who opposed an expansion of the Nicene Creed to include a confession of the Spirit's deity during this era would become known as Pneumatomachi, "fighters against the Spirit," a word coinage based on Acts 5:39.

Basil's classic study of the deity of the Holy Spirit played a pivotal role in shaping the third article of the Niceno-Constantinopolitan creed, but only slowly did he concede that an expansion of the Nicene Creed was necessary so as to include a statement about the deity of the Holy Spirit. Eventually, though, he could note in a letter written in 376 or 377 to Epiphanius (*c.*315–403), the

---

[14] For an excellent study of Basil's life and thought, see Paul Jonathan Fedwick, *The Church and the Charisma of Leadership in Basil of Caesarea* (Toronto: Pontifical Institute of Mediaeval Studies, 1979), 133-155. A more recent work by Philip Rousseau, *Basil of Caesarea* (Berkeley: University of California Press, 1998) needs to be used with care. For a complete bibliography of works on Basil, see Paul Jonathan Fedwick, *Bibliotheca Basiliana Universalis. A Study of the Manuscript Tradition, Translations and Editions of the Works of Basil of Caesarea.* Vol. V: *Studies of Basil of Caesarea and His World: An Annotated Bio-Bibliography* (Turnhout: Brepols, 2004).

bishop of Salamis: "We are unable to add anything to the Nicene creed, not even the smallest addition, except the glorification of the Holy Spirit, because our fathers made mention of this part [of the faith] cursorily, since at that time no controversial question concerning it had yet arisen."[15] In the end this need to expand the article about the Holy Spirit involved the drafting of a new creedal statement at the Council of Constantinople, which was and still is a major landmark in Christian theological reflection.[16]

Although some historians have argued that this fourth-century creedal statement and the earlier one at Nicaea represents the apex of the Hellenization of the church's teaching, in which fourth-century Christianity traded the vitality of the New Testament church's experience of God for a cold, abstract philosophical formula, nothing could be further from the truth.[17] The Niceno-Constantinopolitan creed helped to sum up a long process of reflection that had its origins in the Christian communities of the first century. The New Testament itself provides clear warrant for the direction that theological reflection upon the nature of God took in fourth-century Christian orthodoxy. As Douglas Ottati, an American professor of theology once put it, "Trinitarian theology continues a biblically initiated exploration."[18] Or, in the words of the early twentieth-century theologian, the American

---

[15] *Letter* 258.2. Basil's book is *On the Holy Spirit*, published in 375. For a contemporary translation, see Basil of Caesarea, *On the Holy Spirit*, trans. David Anderson (Crestwood: St Vladimir's Seminary Press, 1980).

[16] For the text of this creed, see J. N. D. Kelly, *Early Christian Creeds* (2nd ed.; London: Longmans, Green and Co Ltd., 1960), 297–298. See also Johannes Roldanus, *The Church in the Age of Constantine: The theological challenges* (Abingdon/New York: Routledge, 2006), 123–126.

[17] Stephen M. Hildebrand identifies Edwin Hatch and Adolf von Harnack as two of the scholars who argued along these lines. See his *The Trinitarian Theology of Basil of Caesarea: A Synthesis of Greek Thought and Biblical Truth* (Washington: Catholic University of America Press, 2007), 7.

[18] "Being trinitarian: The shape of saving faith," *The Christian Century* 112, No. 32 (November 8, 1995): 1045.

Presbyterian Benjamin B. Warfield: the "doctrine of the Trinity lies in Scripture in solution; when it is crystallized from its solvent it does not cease to be Scriptural, but only comes into clearer view."[19]

This biblical foundation of the creed is especially true of the third article that deals with the Holy Spirit. Technical theological terminology as found in the use of the term "one in being" (*homoousios*) about the Son is eschewed in favor of simpler biblical tones.[20] In the words of the Creed, the Holy Spirit in whom the Church believes is:

> The Lord and the giver of life, who proceeds from the Father [and the Son]. With the Father and the Son he is worshipped and glorified. He has spoken through the Prophets.

The statement makes five distinct affirmations about the Holy Spirit:

1. He is Lord (*kyrios*)
2. He is the Giver of Life
3. He proceeds from the Father [and the Son]
4. Together with the Father and the Son he is to be worshipped and glorified
5. And he spoke through the prophets.

Let us look at each of these affirmations in turn, seeking to display the biblical roots of what is being affirmed.

---

[19] "The Biblical Doctrine of the Trinity" in his *Biblical and Theological Studies*, ed. Samuel G. Craig (Philadelphia: The Presbyterian and Reformed Publishing Co., 1952), 22.

[20] Joseph D. Small, "The Spirit and the Creed" in his ed., *Fire and Wind: The Holy Spirit in the Church Today* (Louisville: Geneva Press, 2002), 9.

The Lord

The term *kyrios*, which here is translated "Lord" had a range of meaning in early Christian Greek. It could mean simply an "owner," and is probably used this way in a passage like Matthew 20:8, where it is used to describe "the owner of the vineyard." It can identify a human "master" of slaves, as in passages in the household tables of Ephesians, Colossians, Titus and 1 Peter.[21] And then it is the word used to translate the Hebrew name of God, YHWH, in the Greek Old Testament, and as such is a divine title.[22] In the New Testament, this word is particularly used to describe the Son, as in the phrase "the Lord Jesus Christ," and as such is an indicator of Jesus' divinity. Basil of Caesarea, in his *On the Holy Spirit* (375), noted above, highlights the fact that the New Testament's description of the Holy Spirit as *kyrios*, found in 2 Corinthians 3:17–18,[23] means that the Holy Spirit shares a divine title properly ascribed only to the Father and the Son. For Basil, there are only two types of beings in the universe: God, who is *kyrios*, and everything else, which are God's creatures and, by extension, his servants. If the Spirit is called *kyrios*, as the verses in 2 Corinthians 3 reveal, then he must be as divine as the Father and the Son.[24]

"The giver of life"

The opening verses of the Old Testament, Genesis 1:1–2, indicate that the Spirit was present at and involved in God's creation of this world. Other verses in the Old Testament, such as Job 33:4

---

[21] See, e.g. Ephesians 6:5, 9; Colossians 3:22; 4:1; Titus 2:9; 1 Peter 2:18.

[22] *Early Christian Creeds* (2nd ed.), 341–342.

[23] For a contemporary defense that this classical patristic interpretation of 2 Corinthians 3:17 is correct, see Gordon D. Fee, *God's Empowering Presence: The Holy Spirit in the Letters of Paul* (Peabody: Hendrickson, 1994), 311–314.

[24] *On the Holy Spirit* 21.52.

and Psalm 104:30, denote the Spirit as the One who creates life and sustains all that he has made. In the New Testament, the Spirit is also identified as One who resurrects the dead.[25] But the focus here in the Creed may well be more on the idea of the Holy Spirit as the author of spiritual life, the One who regenerates those who put their faith in Christ, and then sustains them as believers.[26] Relevant biblical texts in this case would be not only statements like that of Jesus in John 6:63, "it is the Spirit who gives life" and Paul's words in 2 Corinthians 3:6, "the Spirit gives life,"[27] but also passages like 1 Corinthians 12:3, where Paul tells us that confession of Christ as Lord can only truly happen when the Holy Spirit implants such a conviction in the heart and mind of a person.

Or consider Titus 3:3–6, where Paul gives his Christian readers a particularly vivid description of the way both he and his hearers once were: "foolish, disobedient, deceived, serving [that is, enslaved to] [various] lusts and pleasures, living in malice and envy, hateful, and hating one another."[28] Totally unable to extricate themselves from this state, it was God alone who enabled them to break free. And one aspect of this saving work is that God saved them "by the washing of regeneration and renewing of the Holy Spirit, whom He poured out on us richly through Jesus Christ our Savior."[29] While this phrase "the washing of regeneration and renewing of the Holy Spirit" has been the subject of

---

[25] Romans 8:11.

[26] A. de Halleux, "La Profession de l'Esprit-Saint dans le symbole de Constantinople," *Revue Théologique de Louvain* 10 (1979): 27; Wolf-Dieter Hauschild, "Das trinitarische Dogma von 381 als Ergebnis verbindlicher Konsensusbildung" in K. Lehmann and W. Pannenberg, eds., *Glaubensbekenntnis und Kirchgemeinschaft: Das Modell des Konzils von Konstantinopel (381)* (Freiburg im Breisau: Herder/Göttingen: Vandenhoeck & Ruprecht, 1982), 35.

[27] See also Galatians 5:25; Romans 8:10.

[28] KJV.

[29] NASB.

much debate in the history of the Church, it is probably best understood as that inner cleansing which the Holy Spirit effects when he regenerates and renews the mind and heart of the new convert.[30] If the Spirit can make dead sinners alive in Christ, however, he must surely be divine.

"Who proceeds from the Father"

One of the great challenges for the Ancient Church in its enunciation of the doctrine of the Trinity was avoiding the heresy of modalism, which appeared in the early third century, about a hundred years or so before the Arian controversy broke out.[31] Modalism, or Sabellianism as it is sometimes known, so named because of a prominent teacher of this error, Sabellius, taught that the differences between the three persons of the Godhead was primarily functional. There is one God who plays three roles, as it were. This view had the benefit of upholding the deity of the Father, Son, and Holy Spirit, but it did so at the dreadful cost of making the biblical witness about the three persons incomprehensible. We are told, for example, in Hebrews 9:14 that Christ "through the eternal Spirit offered himself without blemish to God."[32] How can this verse make any sense if the three persons are really only one person playing three roles? But if, as is the case, there are truly Three within the Godhead, then this verse tells us that, at its heart, the crucifixion of Christ is about the Son making propitiation to the Father, placating his wrath with regard to sin, and that

---

[30] See James D. G. Dunn, *Baptism in the Holy Spirit. A re-examination of the New Testament Teaching on the Gift of the Spirit in relation to Pentecostalism today* (London: SCM Press Ltd., 1970), 165–170.

[31] On modalism, see G.W.H. Lampe, "Christian Theology in the Patristic Period" in Herbert Cunliffe-Jones with Benjamin Drewery, eds., *A History of Christian Doctrine* (1978 ed.; repr. Philadelphia: Fortress Press, 1980), 53–58; Franz Dünzl, *A Brief History of the Doctrine of the Trinity in the Early Church*, trans. John Bowden (London/New York: T&T Clark, 2007), 28–34.

[32] ESV.

Christ did this by the power of the Father's eternal Holy Spirit. What mysteries of holiness and love lie embedded in this text! But all of this is lost in the modalist schema.

Now, from its third-century battles with modalism, the Ancient Church learned that it needed to hold fast to the distinction of the three persons within the Godhead. She did so by means of phrases that can be seen in this Creed: the Father differs from the Son and the Spirit in that he is unbegotten. The Son differs from the Father and the Spirit for he is eternally begotten. And the Spirit's distinctiveness is found in his eternal proceeding from the Father. As Harold O.J. Brown, who taught for many years at Trinity Evangelical Divinity School, rightly notes: "Ultimately this language tells us…that the Father, the Son, and the Holy Spirit are distinct Persons" and makes clear that in "the Trinity we are dealing with three distinctive Persons, not merely with modes or appearances of one and the same Person."[33]

Biblical support for the Spirit's eternal procession was found by authors like Basil of Caesarea in such Scripture texts as John 15:26, 1 Corinthians 2:12, and Psalm 33:6. Basil employed these to argue that the Spirit "proceeds from the mouth of the Father and is not begotten like the Son."[34] Basil quickly qualified this image. The terms "breath" and "mouth" must be understood in a manner befitting to God. The comparison of the Spirit with breath does not mean that he is the same as human breath, which quickly dissipates upon exhalation, for the Spirit is a living being with the power to sanctify others. This image well reflects the nature of our knowledge about God. On the one hand, it indicates the intimate relationship of the Father and the Spirit so the Spirit has to be

---

[33] Harold O.J. Brown, *Heresies* (Garden City: Doubleday & Co., Inc., 1984), 133.

[34] *On the Holy Spirit* 18.46, trans. David Anderson, *St Basil the Great: On the Holy Spirit* (Crestwood: St. Vladimir's Seminary Press, 1980), 73. See also *On the Holy Spirit* 16.38.

glorified with the Father and the Son. On the other hand, the image reminds us that the Spirit's mode of existence is ineffable, even as the being of the Godhead is beyond human comprehension.

"With the Father and the Son he is worshipped and glorified"
As the Patristic scholar J.N.D. Kelly has put it, this is the "all-important clause."[35] It is inconceivable that someone who denied the deity of the Spirit could have subscribed to this statement.[36] The logic would appear to be this: if it is right and proper that the Spirit be adored and glorified on the same level as the Father and the Son, then he must be fully God.

The wording of this statement is clearly indebted to Basil of Caesarea, who in his classic work *On the Holy Spirit* had argued for the co-adoration and co-glorification of the Spirit with the Father and the Son. Basil's opponents, the Pneumatomachi were maintaining that it was proper only to give glory to the Father *through* the Son *in* the Holy Spirit. A specific question had come to Basil from his close friend Amphilochius of Iconium (*c.*340-395), whom he had mentored, asking whether or not it was also proper in corporate worship to glorify the Father *with* the Son *together with* the Holy Spirit.[37]

The core of Basil's book, *On the Holy Spirit* 10–28, was essentially a detailed exposition of much of the biblical testimony about the Spirit's person to demonstrate the deity of the Spirit and thus the rightness of his co-adoration and co-glorification. A number of key themes informed Basil's argument. From the presence of the Spirit in the baptismal formula of Matthew 28, he argued

---

[35] *Early Christian Creeds* (2nd ed.), 342.
[36] See Adolf-Martin Ritter, *Das Konzil von Konstantinopel und sein Symbol* (Göttingen: Vandenhoeck & Ruprecht, 1965), 301.
[37] Basil, *On the Holy Spirit* 1.1, 3.

that the mention of "Father, Son, and Spirit" in this formula "testifies to their union and fellowship." Thus he went on to state, "The Lord has delivered to us a necessary and saving dogma: the Holy Spirit is to be ranked with the Father."[38] Then, from a variety of biblical texts that speak of the Spirit's activities Basil showed how the Spirit "is indivisibly and inseparably joined to the Father and the Son" since he does what only God can do. The Spirit sanctifies the angels, for example, and enables them to remain steadfast in their allegiance to God, something he could not do unless he were divine. The holiness of the angels is not inherent, but results from their communion with One who is innately holy, namely the Spirit:

> How can the Seraphim sing, "Holy, holy, holy," without the Spirit teaching them to constantly raise their voices in praise? If all God's angels praise him, and all His host, they do so by cooperating with the Spirit. Do a thousand thousands of angels serve him? Do ten thousand times ten thousand stand before him? They accomplish their proper work by the Spirit's power.[39]

Basil also pointed to the titles given by Scripture to the Spirit to argue for his deity. For instance, the ascription of the term "Lord" to the Spirit—which has been discussed above—was indisputable proof of the "excellence of the Spirit's glory."[40] It is noteworthy that Basil did not explicitly call the Spirit "God" nor did he speak of the Spirit as "one in being" (*homoousios*) with the

---

[38] Basil, *On the Holy Spirit* 10.24, 25, trans. Anderson, *On the Holy Spirit*, 45, 46.
[39] Basil, *On the Holy Spirit* 16.37, 38, trans. Anderson, *On the Holy Spirit*, 60, 64.
[40] Basil, *On the Holy Spirit* 21.52.

Father and the Son, although it is very clear that he was committed to both of these truths.[41]

Then, the Spirit is the one who gives saving knowledge of God, but only God can reveal God. In Basil's words:

> When, by means of the illuminating power, we fix our eyes on the beauty of the invisible image and through that image are led up to the supremely beautiful spectacle of the Archetype, the Spirit of knowledge is inseparably present there [with the Father and the Son]. To those who love the vision of the truth the Spirit supplies in himself the power to behold the image. He does not give the revelation from without, but in himself leads to the knowledge [of the image]. For just as "no one knows the Father except the Son" [Matthew 11:27], so "no one can say Jesus is Lord except in the Holy Spirit" [1 Corinthians 12:3]. For it does not say "through the Spirit" but "in the Spirit." … And, as it is written, "in your light we shall see light" [Psalm 36:9], that is, in the illumination of the Spirit [we shall see] "the true light that enlightens every man that comes into the world" [John 1:9]. Thus, in himself he makes known the glory of the Only-Begotten, and in himself provides the knowledge of God to the true worshippers. Therefore, the way of the knowledge of God is from the one Spirit through the one Son to the one Father.[42]

Here Basil is building on such passages as Hebrews 1:3 and Colossians 1:15 in which the Son is described as the image of the Father, whom Basil calls the "Archetype." During the course of the Arian

---

[41] John Behr, *The Nicene Faith. Volume 2. Part Two: One of the Holy Trinity* (Crestwood: St Vladimir's Seminary Press, 2004), 378.

[42] Basil, *On the Holy Spirit* 18.47, trans. Michael A.G. Haykin. See also *On the Holy Spirit* 26.64 for similar argumentation.

controversy, it had become a commonplace to argue that the Son's being the image of the Father meant that there was a community of nature between the Son and the Father. But knowledge of the image and by extension its Archetype is impossible without the Spirit who reveals the Son—here Basil is drawing upon 1 Corinthians 12:3. Moreover, this knowledge is given by the Spirit "in himself." Knowledge of God does not come through an intermediary like an angel, but is given by God by/in himself, namely in the Spirit, who must therefore be divine. This text then tells us why the Spirit is inextricably joined to the Father and the Son. His epistemic relationship to the Father and the Son speaks of an ontological union.[43] As Basil noted in one of his letters: "Therefore we never divorce the Paraclete from his unity with the Father and the Son; for our mind when it is lit by the Spirit looks up to the Son and in him as in an image beholds the Father."[44]

"He has spoken through the Prophets"

The Scriptural basis for this final remark is 2 Peter 1:20–21, where the inspiration of the Old Testament Scriptures is ascribed to the Holy Spirit.[45] This phrase recalls the theology of the prophetic Spirit that was a major feature of second-century Christian thought about the Holy Spirit and that especially sought to refute the rejection of the Old Testament by heretics like Marcion.[46] But

---

[43] Hildebrand, *Trinitarian Theology of Basil of Caesarea*, 187, 190–191.

[44] Basil, *Letter* 226.3, trans. Michael A.G. Haykin. It is because of the Scriptural witness and the reasoning of the Fathers that I find C.F.D. Moule's statement that "threefoldness is, perhaps, less vital to a Christian conception of God than the eternal twofoldness of Father and Son" completely unsatisfactory (*The Holy Spirit* [1978 ed.; repr. London/New York: Continuum, 2000], 51). There is much that is good in this book by Moule, but his chapter dealing with the development of Trinitarianism in the post-Apostolic church, of which the above statement is the concluding remark, is not helpful.

[45] Also see Ephesians 3:5; 2 Timothy 3:16–17.

[46] De Halleux, "Profession de l'Esprit-Saint," 30–31. For examples of the second-century theology of the prophetic Spirit, see Theophilus, *To Autolycus* 2.9; Athenagoras,

why was it affirmed in this creedal statement? It is noteworthy that Basil could describe the inspiration of the whole Bible, both the Old and the New Testaments, as prophetic.[47] Undoubtedly, he considered the prophetism of the Scriptures a proof of the divinity of the Spirit who inspired them.[48]

The deity of the Holy Spirit

It is quite probable that one of the leading figures behind the com-position of this creedal statement was Basil's younger brother, Gregory of Nyssa (*c.*335–*c.*395), for Gregory had drunk deeply from the well of both Scripture and his brother's doctrine of the Spirit.[49] There is, however, one aspect of New Testament pneu-matology that is missing from this paragraph on the Spirit, namely the fact that, in the New Testament, the Holy Spirit is ever the Spirit of Christ.[50] This lacuna is probably one of the key impulses behind the development of the *filioque*, that is, the addition to this confession by Latin-speaking Christians in the early Middle Ages that the Holy Spirit "proceeds from the Father and the Son."[51] I personally think that this addition is correct,[52] which also high-lights the fact that the Niceno-Constantinopolitan Creed must be viewed as a *norma normata*, "a rule that is ruled," not a *norma nor-mans*, "a rule that rules," as Roman Catholic and Orthodox theo-logians assert when they postulate that this creed along with other

---

Plea for the Christians 10.4; Irenaeus, *Demonstration of the Apostolic Preaching* 49; L.W. Bar-nard, *Justin Martyr* (Cambridge: Cambridge University Press, 1967), 102–103.

[47] Hildebrand, *Trinitarian Theology of Basil of Caesarea*, 109–114.

[48] De Halleux, "Profession de l'Esprit-Saint," 31.

[49] See Michael A.G. Haykin, *The Spirit of God: The Exegesis of 1 and 2 Corinthians in the Pneumatomachian Controversy of the Fourth Century* (Leiden: E.J. Brill, 1994), 193–201.

[50] See, for example, Acts 16:7; Romans 8:9; 2 Corinthians 3:17; Galatians 4:6; and those passages that describe Jesus as the giver, or associated with the gift, of the Spirit: John 14:26; 15:26; 16:7, 14; 20:22; Acts 2:33; Titus 3:6.

[51] Jenson, "Holy Spirit" in *Christian Dogmatics*, 2:121.

[52] In this regard, see Dennis Ngien's fine study, *Apologetic for Filioque in Medieval The-ology* (Milton Keynes: Paternoster, 2005).

ancient creeds, is of absolute authority and infallible. Creeds are not infallible. Like other human formulations the creeds are subordinate to Scripture, the supreme rule of faith and practice. As Bruce Demarest has put it, the creeds "are worthy of honour to the degree that they accord with the teachings of the Word of God."[53] On the other hand, this pneumatological statement, like the rest of the creed, is a rule that faithfully reflects the view of God in the New Testament. And as such, it stands as one of the great landmarks of Christian theology.[54]

It is in the spirit of my approach to this creed—not infallible but utterly vital for theological health—that the rest of the chapters are written. I am seeking to reflect on what it means to live in the Spirit, given that he is God and worthy of our adoration, and to do so in light of the infallible Word of God and the way that that Word has been interpreted in the history of the Church.

---

[53] Bruce A. Demarest, "The contemporary relevance of Christendom's creeds," *Themelios* 7, no. 2 (January 1982): 15–16.
[54] Demarest, "Christendom's creeds," 15.

2
THE GIFT OF THE HOLY SPIRIT

*No words are adequate to express the excellence
and dignity of the gift of the divine Spirit.*

Robert Hall, Jr.
(1764–1831)

Margaret Visser, the bestselling essayist who used to teach classics at York University, has observed that the constant use of "thank you" in the speech of English-speaking people appears quite odd to people from certain other language groups. The latter become suspicious if they keep hearing "thanks" and "thank you" from English speakers and suspect them of using the phrases to impress or to hide other motives.[1] Now, could it be the case that this habit of saying "thank you" by Anglophones—a typical English speaker can say "thank you" up to a hundred times or more a day[2]—has been formed by biblical categories of thinking? Not only are there admonitions to be grateful in the Bible,[3] but the Bible frequently shows us thanksgiving in action. The Apostle Paul's customary practice, for instance, at the beginning of his letters to include a thanksgiving to God for those to whom he was writing. Consider Ephesians 1:3–14, for example.

---

[1] *The Gift of Thanks. The Roots, Persistence, and Paradoxical Meanings of a Social Ritual* (Toronto: Harper Collins Publishers Ltd., 2008), 7.

[2] Visser, *Gift of Thanks*, 8.

[3] See, for instance, Psalm 118:29; 1 Thessalonians 5:18; Ephesians 5:20.

Unlike the rest of Paul's letters, the letter to the Ephesians is what we could call a circular letter, addressed to a number of churches in Ephesus and the surrounding region.[4] Because of this, Paul gives thanks for what is common to all Christians, all of the gifts that God the Father has given to those who are in Christ:

- The utterly unmerited gift of being chosen for salvation (verse 4)
- The privilege of being adopted as a child of God (verse 5)
- The amazing grace of being redeemed (verse 7)
- The sheer favor bound up in the forgiveness of sins (verse 7)
- The ever-practical present of wisdom and spiritual insight (verses 8–9)
- The gift of the promised Holy Spirit (verses 13–14).

Each of these could form the centrepiece of a rewarding study, but in this chapter we want to focus on the final one, the "gift of the Holy Spirit" as outlined by Paul in Ephesians 1:13–14:

> In him you also, when you heard the word of truth, the gospel of your salvation, and believed in him, were sealed with the promised Holy Spirit, who is the guarantee of our inheritance until we acquire possession of it, to the praise of his glory.[5]

---

[4] G. Zuntz, *The Text of the Epistles. A Disquisition upon the Corpus Paulinum* (London: Oxford University Press, 1953), 228, n.1; F.F. Bruce, *The Epistle to the Ephesians* (London: Pickering & Inglis Ltd., 1961), 26; Ernest Best, "Ephesians i.1" in his and R. McL. Wilson, eds., *Texts and Interpretation. Studies in the New Testament presented to Matthew Black* (Cambridge: Cambridge University Press, 1979), 29–41.

[5] ESV.

The promised Holy Spirit

It was the great Puritan theologian Jonathan Edwards (1703–1758) who often made the point that the great blessing secured by the death of Christ was the gift of the Spirit. "The sum of the blessings Christ sought," wrote Edwards in 1748, "by what he did and suffered in the work of redemption, was the Holy Spirit." As he further argued:

> The Holy Spirit, in his indwelling, his influences and fruits, is the sum of all grace, holiness, comfort and joy, or in one word, of all the spiritual good Christ purchased for men in this world: and is also the sum of all perfection, glory and eternal joy, that he purchased for them in another world.[6]

This gift of supreme goodness had been promised throughout the era of the Old Testament prophets. One thinks of passages like Isaiah 44:3, Ezekiel 36:26–27 and Joel 2:28–29 in this regard, for example. Then, during his ministry the Lord Jesus had promised the coming of the Spirit. In the Upper Room Discourse, for instance, recorded for us in John 14–16, Jesus repeatedly came back to this subject.

Jesus was going to ask the Father to give his disciples an advocate-helper like himself, "even the Spirit of truth," who would be in them forever.[7] One of the reasons that the Father would give them the Spirit was to "teach them all things" and help them remember Christ's doctrine[8] and ultimately bring glory to Christ.[9] In fact, the Father's gift of the Spirit would come through Jesus

---

[6] *Humble Attempt* in *Apocalyptic Writings*, ed. Stephen J. Stein (*The Works of Jonathan Edwards*, vol. 5; New Haven/London: Yale University Press, 1977), 341.

[7] John 14:16–17.

[8] John 14:26; 16:13.

[9] John 16:14.

himself,[10] because the Father had constituted Jesus as the unique Christ (see John 3:34).[11]

After his resurrection, Jesus returned to this subject of the promise of the Spirit, when he acted out what would happen shortly to them. In John 20:22 we are told that he breathed upon his disciples while telling them, "Receive the Holy Spirit." Technically known as insufflation, this acted prophecy drove home what we have already seen from John 14–16, namely that the Father and the Son are co-donors of the gift of the Spirit.[12]

Yet again, according to Luke 24:49, Christ told his disciples before his ascension that he was going to give them "the promise of the Father." But they had to remain in the place where they would receive this great gift, namely Jerusalem. And when the gift of the Spirit was given at Pentecost, the Apostle Peter had no doubt that Jesus' giving them the Spirit has enormous Christological import. To be the giver of the Spirit, Jesus must be none other than the Lord seated at the right hand of God.[13]

The indwelling Spirit

It is vital to note that the coming of the Spirit at Pentecost, the fulfillment of long-awaited expectation, ushered in a radically new age. In fact, so different is this new age from the pre-Pentecost era that John can say that prior to Jesus' glorification in his death, resurrection and ascension, it was if the Spirit "was not yet [given]."[14] Of course, this is not to be understood as a statement

---

[10] John 15:26.

[11] On Jesus as the bestower of the Spirit, see especially Graham A. Cole, *He Who Gives Life: The Doctrine of the Holy Spirit* (Wheaton: Crossway Books, 2007), 179-207. On the teaching about the Spirit in John, see James M. Hamilton, Jr., *God's Indwelling Presence: The Holy Spirit in the Old & New Testaments* (Nashville: B&H Publishing, 2006), 56-99.

[12] Cole, *He Who Gives Life*, 188-191.

[13] Acts 2:33.

[14] John 7:39

about the being of the Spirit. As the Spirit of God, the Holy Spirit is as eternal as the other members of the Godhead. Rather, this statement is about the work of the Holy Spirit: there is a distinct, qualitative difference between his ministry before Pentecost and that after Pentecost.[15]

What was it that was new in the work of the Spirit post-Pentecost? In a nutshell it is this: prior to Pentecost, while the Spirit did regenerate numbers among the people of Israel, he did not indwell them. Consider in this regard John 14:17b. God's dwelling place among his people in the pre-Pentecost era, the Old Testament consistently affirms to be the Temple.[16] On the other hand, central to the new covenant is the promise that the Spirit would indwell all individuals who are among the people of God.[17]

"Sealed with the Spirit"

Now, one key aspect of the Spirit's work in the post-Pentecost era is that he is a seal in the lives of the people of God. When they heard the gospel and believed it, they were "sealed with the Holy Spirit." In Paul's day, seals were employed in a variety of ways. They indicated ownership, for example. Cattle and sheep would be branded with the names of their owner. Slaves who had a habit of running away would be branded with a view to preventing further attempts at escape.[18] Seals were also employed to prove

---

[15] Sinclair B. Ferguson, *The Holy Spirit* (Downers Grove: InterVarsity Press, 1996), 67–68; Hamilton, Jr., *God's Indwelling Presence*, 100–121; Cole, *He Who Gives Life*, 183–184.

[16] Hamilton, Jr., *God's Indwelling Presence*, 163. See the entirety of Hamilton, Jr., *God's Indwelling Presence* for his full argument. For a shorter statement of this position, see Cole, *He Who Gives Life*, 143–145.

[17] Look, for example, at the following representative texts from the New Testament: Romans 5:5; Galatians 4:6; 1 Corinthians 3:16—here the Christian community collectively is viewed as the temple (*naos*) of God; Ephesians 2:19-22

[18] David Ewert, *The Holy Spirit in the New Testament* (Kitchener/Scottsdale: Herald Press, 1983), 283; G.W.H. Lampe, *The Seal of the Spirit. A Study in the Doctrine of Baptism and Confirmation in the New Testament and the Fathers* (London: Longmans, Green and Co.,

authenticity. Deeds of sale were authorized by seals and the emperor would send mail which bore his seal to identify the letters as coming from the imperial hand.[19] In the words of John Calvin, "a seal distinguishes what is true and certain, from what is false and spurious."[20] Finally, seals were a way of making an object secure.[21] And it is probably this meaning that is uppermost in Paul's mind here in Ephesians 1. This is because Paul follows up the statement about the sealing of the Spirit with another image that we shall see also bespeaks security: the gift of the Holy Spirit is like a "downpayment" or "guarantee" of our future inheritance.

Those who are sealed with the Spirit are protected: not against the trials and tribulations of this life—being a Christian does not render one immune from the afflictions and suffering of this world—but against the reality of eternal destruction. Thus Paul warns his first readers in the churches of Ephesus not to "grieve the Holy Spirit of God, by whom you were sealed for the day of redemption."[22] As Richard Sibbes (1577–1635), the Stuart Puritan, noted, "where this seal of the Spirit is, it is an argument that God means to preserve such a one from eternal destruction[.]"[23] The gift of the Spirit to a person is ultimately then a guarantee that he or she will persevere in the faith. The Irish

---

1951), 8–9. See also John Owen, *Of Communion with God the Father, Son, and Holy Ghost* in *The Works of John Owen*, ed. William H. Goold (1850–1853 ed.; repr. Edinburgh: The Banner of Truth Trust, 1965) II, 243.

[19] S.S. Smalley, "Seal, Sealing" in J.D. Douglas *et al.*, eds., *The New Bible Dictionary* (Grand Rapids: Wm. B. Eerdmans, 1962), 1156; Catherine Salles, "Les Postiers Romains," *Historama* 15 (May 1985): 59–60.

[20] *Commentaries on The Epistles of Paul to the Galatians and Ephesians*, trans. William Pringle (Edinburgh: Calvin Translation Society, 1844), 208.

[21] Charles Hodge, *A Commentary on the Epistle to the Ephesians* (London: James Nisbet, 1881), 34–35; Gordon D. Fee, *God's Empowering Presence: The Holy Spirit in the Letters of Paul* (Peabody: Hendrickson, 1994), 292.

[22] Ephesians 4:30 ESV.

[23] *A Fountain Sealed* (1637) in his *The Complete Works of Richard Sibbes* (Edinburgh: James Nichol, 1863), V, 437.

Baptist Alexander Carson (1776–1844) put it well when he stated, "He that is once sealed by the Spirit, is secured to eternity."[24]

The Spirit is the seal, not the Sealer

It is important to note that the Spirit here is regarded as a gift. He is not depicted as the Giver. There have been some respected theologians and Bible scholars who have argued, though, that the Spirit is not to be viewed here as a gift so much as the Giver. In other words, rather than viewing him as a seal and the Father as the Sealer, the Spirit himself should be recognized as the Sealer and a specific experience discussed below as the seal

The Puritan Thomas Goodwin (1600–1679), for instance, argued that the sealing of the Spirit was a post-conversion experience that bespoke assurance of salvation. It was given by the Spirit the Sealer who "cometh and overpowereth a man's soul, and assureth him that God is his, and he is God's, and that God loveth him from everlasting." Goodwin argued his case from the rendering of a part of this verse in the King James Version, which reads thus: "after that ye believed, ye were sealed with that Holy Spirit of promise." Following this translation, Goodwin assumed that the sealing by the Spirit occurred at a point in time after the initial step of faith.[25]

One important twentieth-century preacher who followed this line of argument was D. Martyn Lloyd-Jones (1899–1981), who played one of the key roles in the recovery of Calvinistic truth in our day. The Welsh preacher consistently maintained that the

---

[24] *Baptism in its Mode and Subjects* (5th American ed.; Philadelphia: American Baptist Publication Society, 1860), 235.

[25] *An Exposition of the First Chapter of the Epistle to the Ephesians* in *The Works of Thomas Goodwin* (Edinburgh: James Nichol, 1861), I, 233–238.

sealing of the Spirit was an experience subsequent to conversion.[26] Thus, he believed that a person can be "a Christian without the sealing of the Spirit."[27] Lloyd-Jones found ready support for his view in, among others, the writings of Thomas Goodwin.

But, as Australian scholar Peter T. O'Brien has emphasized: "The participle ["after that ye believed"] does not here express antecedent action, as though the Gentiles believed and then subsequently were sealed with the Holy Spirit. Rather, the believing and being sealed were two sides of the one event."[28] It was at the very moment they believed that they were sealed by God the Father through the gift of the Spirit.[29] And all believers are so sealed with the Spirit. In the text before us, Paul gives no indication that only some of his Ephesian recipients had been sealed with the Spirit. No, it is a reality for all who put their faith in Christ. When they believe, they are sealed.

Incidentally, Paul's clear conviction that the Spirit is given when men and women simply believe stood in strong contrast to the rabbinic teaching of the Ancient World. Read the following words of Rabbi Phinehas ben Jair (*fl.*165–200):

> The Torah leads to watchfulness, watchfulness to diligence, diligence to cleanliness, cleanliness to self-control, self-control to purity, purity to piety, piety to humility, humility to fear of sin, fear of sin to holiness, holiness to the Holy Spirit, the Holy Spirit to the resurrection of the dead.[30]

---

[26] *God's Ultimate Purpose: An Exposition of Ephesians 1, 1–23* (Edinburgh: Banner of Truth Trust, 1978), 248–254.

[27] *God's Ultimate Purpose*, 266.

[28] *The Letter to the Ephesians* (Grand Rapids/Cambridge: Wm. B. Eerdmans/Leicester: Apollos, 1999), 119 and nn. 125–126.

[29] Dunn, *Baptism in the Holy Spirit*, 158–159.

[30] Cited W.D. Davies, *Paul and Rabbinic Judaism: Some Rabbinic Elements of Pauline Theology* (1955 ed.; Repr. New York/Evanston: Harper & Row, Publishers, 1967), 209.

According to this passage, which is typical of rabbinic thought, the Spirit's presence must be earned. How different the grace-centered teaching of Paul! Not because of good works that we have done, but on the basis of God's kindness and mercy do we receive the Spirit when we believe.

The Spirit as a "pledge"

It was customary for the rabbis of Paul's day to think of the activity of the Holy Spirit as belonging to the past. For the rabbis, the Spirit had been active in the history of Israel, giving her the Torah and speaking through the prophets. But, it was said, "when the last prophets Haggai, Zechariah and Malachi died the Holy Spirit ceased out of Israel."[31] Yet, these very same religious leaders also cherished a strong hope that in the future, when Messiah came to establish the Messianic Age, it would again be a period in which the Spirit would be active. They fully expected that the Age to come or the Messianic era would also be an Age of the Spirit.[32]

Well, what these rabbis longed for had happened through the life and ministry, through the death and resurrection of the Lord Jesus Christ. The future has, as it were, come back into the present, and the Spirit, who would rule in the Age to Come, was now active in the present, a witness to the reality of Christ's Messiahship and a powerful foretaste of even greater yet to come. Now, one of the ways in which the Apostle Paul describes the Spirit's work in this regard is to call him "a pledge" (*arrhabōn*).[33] This Greek word that Paul uses was actually a loan-word from the Phoenician world and originally had the idea of a precious article that was given by a debtor to a creditor as a guarantee of future

---

[31] Cited Davies, *Paul and Rabbinic Judaism*, 209.

[32] Davies, *Paul and Rabbinic Judaism*, 215–216.

[33] The Spirit is so described in three Pauline passages: 2 Corinthians 1:22; 5:5; and Ephesians 1:14.

payments and that would be given back when the debt was paid. In time, the word also came to indicate a "down payment" of money against a loan that ensured future payments but also reduced the amount of indebtedness. Most commentators would argue that it is the latter idea that is in Paul's mind as he uses this metaphor of the Holy Spirit. The experience of the Spirit in this life is a guarantee of a much richer experience in the life to come.

The early Christian theologian Irenaeus of Lyons captures Paul's thought here perfectly when he wrote around the year 180:

> We have now received a certain portion of his Spirit, ... which the apostle also terms "a guarantee," ... [as] he says in the Epistle to the Ephesians, "In him you also, when you heard the word of truth, the gospel of your salvation, and believed in him, were sealed with the promised Holy Spirit, who is the guarantee of our inheritance." This guarantee, therefore, thus dwelling in us, renders us spiritual even now... For those to whom [Paul] was writing were ... those who had received the Spirit of God, "by which we cry, Abba, Father" [Romans 8:15]. If therefore, at the present time, having the guarantee, we do cry, "Abba, Father," what shall it be when, on rising again, we behold him face to face, when all the members [of his Body] shall burst out into a continuous hymn of triumph, glorifying him who raised them from the dead, and gave them the gift of eternal life?[34]

No matter how great the experience of the Spirit in this world, a much richer experience in the age to come awaits those whom he indwells. And then the ultimate purpose of the gift of

---

[34] *Against Heresies* 5.8.1, trans. Alexander Roberts and W.H. Rambaut in A. Cleveland Coxe, arr., *The Apostolic Fathers with Justin Martyr and Irenaeus* (Ante-Nicene Fathers, vol. 1; 1885 ed.; repr. New York: Charles Scribner's Sons, 1903), 533, altered.

the Holy Spirit will be realized—"when all the members [of the Body of Christ] shall burst out into a continuous hymn of triumph, glorifying him who raised them from the dead, and gave them the gift of eternal life."

3

"The Spirit of holiness": The sanctifying work of the Holy Spirit[1]

Can a man have the Holy Spirit, and not love holiness?

John Ryland, Jr.
(1753–1825)

The holiness of the Holy Spirit

In a study of the concept of holiness in the ancient world, Hannah K. Harrington maintained that for pre-Christian and first-century Judaism, "holiness describes God more closely than any other designation. His very essence is holiness. One could say that holiness is God's 'innermost reality' to which all of His attributes are related."[2] To describe God as holy was, for these Jews, to speak of his transcendent perfection and his "exalted, powerful otherness that brings people to both admire and fear him."[3] Inextricably linked to this description, in their minds, was also the conviction that God is omnibenevolent. In all of his doings God is utterly

---

[1] This chapter originated as a paper at "Our Holy God," a conference sponsored by the Alliance of Confessing Evangelicals, Nassau Christian Center, Princeton, October 27, 2007. With some modifications it was also given as an address at the Evangelical Movement of Wales Ministers' Conference, Bala, Wales, June 16, 2008.

[2] *Holiness: Rabbinic Judaism and the Graeco-Roman World* (London/New York: Routledge, 2001), 11–12. This study is a tremendous resource in exploring ideological aspects of the New Testament background as it relates to the concept of holiness.

[3] Harrington, *Holiness*, 27, 13.

41

beneficent and wholly righteous in his exercise of justice and mercy.[4]

When the New Testament, therefore, describes the Spirit of God as the "Holy Spirit," "the Spirit, the Holy One,"[5] or as Romans 1:4 puts it, "the Spirit of holiness," a profound statement is being made about the nature of the Spirit. Since innate holiness belongs only to God, to call the Spirit "holy" is to imply that he is holy by nature and must be divine. There is, however, no extended discussion in the New Testament of the Spirit's nature. But in the three centuries immediately following the Apostolic era this subject was raised and an answer that was ultimately shaped by Scripture given: the Spirit is fully God and worthy of divine honors. It fell especially to the fourth-century Cappadocian Fathers—Basil of Caesarea, his brother Gregory of Nyssa, their close friend Gregory of Nazianzus, and Nazianzen's cousin Amphilochius of Iconium—to elucidate for the Church the biblical data regarding the person of the Holy Spirit. As we have seen in Chapter 1, Basil's superb defense of the propriety of worshipping the Spirit in his important treatise *On the Holy Spirit* (375) led directly to the third article of the creedal statement issued at the Council of Constantinople (381) in which, among other things, it was confessed: "We

---

[4] Harrington, *Holiness*, 27–44, *passim*.

[5] See, for example, 1 Thessalonians 4:8 or Ephesians 4:30. By contrast, it is noteworthy that the application of the term "holy" to the Spirit in either the Old Testament or inter-testamental Judaism is not frequent. It occurs in only three places in the Old Testament—Psalm 51:11; Isaiah 63:10 and 11. When it is found in inter-testamental Judaism it refers more often than not to a "God-given disposition to holiness" and principle of obedience, and not the Spirit of God. See Barry D. Smith, "Pauline Studies: Pauline Pneumatology" (http://www.abu.nb.ca/courses/pauline/Spirit.htm; accessed October 22, 2007) and his "The Spirit of Holiness as Eschatological Principle of Obedience in Second-Temple Judaism" (http://www.abu.nb.ca/courses/pauline/SpirHol.htm; accessed October 22, 2007).

Harrington suggests that the reason why "the Rabbis do not refer overly much to the Holy Spirit" is due to the Spirit's "strong personification as a separate divine being in early Christianity" (*Holiness*, 32).

believe in the Holy Spirit, the Lord and giver of life,…who together with the Father and the Son is adored and glorified." And, as we also noted in that chapter, there is every reason to believe that Basil's younger brother, Gregory was asked to draw up this article.[6]

Now, the connection between the Spirit's innate holiness and his deity is clearly brought out in a letter that Basil wrote in 373:

> We glorify the Holy Spirit together with the Father and the Son, from the conviction that he is not separated from the divine nature: what is foreign by nature does not share in the same honors. … [For] the creature is sanctified; the Spirit sanctifies. Whether you name angels, archangels, or all the heavenly powers, they receive their sanctification through the Spirit, but the Spirit has his holiness by nature, not as received by grace, but essentially his. From this, he has received the distinctive name of Holy. What then is by nature holy, as the Father is by nature holy and the Son by nature holy, we do not allow to be separated and severed from the divine and blessed Trinity.[7]

At the heart of this argument for the divine transcendence of the Spirit is the fact that he sanctifies others, for only that which is holy by nature—and thus divine—can sanctify another.

On the other hand, if one inquires as to what the New Testament teaches about the Spirit's sanctifying work, there is an abundance of material that could be examined. In what follows, key

---

[6] For a discussion of the pneumatological achievement of the Cappadocian Fathers, see Michael A.G. Haykin, *The Spirit of God: The Exegesis of 1 and 2 Corinthians in the Pneumatomachian Controversy of the Fourth Century* (Leiden: E. J. Brill, 1994), *passim.*

[7] *Letter* 159.2 in J. Patout Burns and Gerald M. Fagin, *The Holy Spirit* (Message of the Fathers of the Church, vol. 3; Wilmington, Delaware: Michael Glazer, Inc., 1984), 122.

texts from two letters in the Pauline corpus—Romans and 1 Thessalonians—serve as the basis of a discussion of the Holy Spirit as the giver of holiness.

The Spirit of holiness

One does not have to read far in Romans—the most systematic of all of Paul's letters—to encounter a reference to the Spirit's sanctifying work. In Romans 1:4 Paul describes the Spirit with a phrase that is unique in the New Testament—he is the "Spirit of holiness."[8] What exactly does the Apostle mean by describing the Spirit thus? Why does he not use the more common term "Holy Spirit"? For some writers the terms "Holy Spirit" and "Spirit of holiness" are simply synonymous and they would understand the term "Spirit of holiness" to mean something like "the Spirit whose character is holiness." There is another way, though, to understand this phrase and that is to see it as a description of the Spirit's work: he is the giver of holiness, the One who supplies holiness to all who call upon the name of Jesus.[9] Given the Old Testament form of the phrase "Spirit of holiness," the latter interpretation is probably the better of the two. It highlights the fact that central among the activities of the Spirit is the sanctification of the people of God. In fact, for Paul as for the other New Testament authors, the Holy Spirit is indispensable for living a life that pleases God.[10]

---

[8] As James D.G. Dunn notes, the term "Spirit of holiness" would almost certainly be understood by Paul and the first Christians as denoting the Holy Spirit" (*Romans 1–8* [Word Biblical Commentary, vol. 38A; Dallas: Word Publishing, 1988], 14-15). See also Thomas R. Schreiner, *Romans* (Grand Rapids: Baker, 1998), 43.

[9] C.E.B. Cranfield, *Romans: A Shorter Commentary* (Grand Rapids: Wm. B. Eerdmans, 1985), 7; Gordon D. Fee, *God's Empowering Presence: The Holy Spirit in the Letters of Paul* (Peabody: Hendrickson, 1994), 483.

[10] See Smith, "Pauline Studies: Pauline Pneumatology."

Another key text with regard to the Spirit's sanctifying work is found in Romans 15:8–21. Here, the Apostle begins by indicating that one of the ultimate goals of Christ's ministry was that Gentiles might come to glorify the God of Israel for being a God of mercy. The citation of four Old Testament texts, drawn from various parts of the Old Testament canon, supports this affirmation.[11] Christ's intentions with regard to the Gentiles is of central concern to the Apostle for he has been called by God to preach Christ among the Gentiles where the name of Jesus has never been heard,[12] or, as he puts it earlier, "to be a minister of Christ Jesus to the Gentiles in the priestly service of the gospel of God."[13] Using imagery drawn from the Temple worship of Israel to describe his ministry, Paul argues that Gentiles—who were formerly ritually impure and thus utterly unacceptable to God—have now become acceptable to God. In the immediate context of these verses, what has made them acceptable is their embrace of the gospel, which, in turn, was made possible by the Holy Spirit's power.[14] In Paul's words, they have been "sanctified by the Holy Spirit,"[15] that is, set apart to serve God and to fulfill his purposes, which, because of God's holy character, inevitably involves leading lives of godliness.[16] It is on the basis of this sanctifying work of the Spirit that Paul, later in this chapter and in the one that follows, can call believers "saints."[17]

---

[11] Romans 15:8–12.

[12] Romans 15:20.

[13] Romans 15:16 ESV.

[14] Romans 15:19.

[15] Romans 15:16.

[16] See the similar idea in 1 Corinthians 6:11. See also the comments of James D.G. Dunn, *Romans 9–16* (Word Biblical Commentary, vol. 38B; Dallas: Word, 1988), 860–861; Fee, *God's Empowering Presence*, 626–627; David Peterson, *Possessed by God. A New Testament Theology of Sanctification and Holiness* (Grand Rapids: Wm. B. Eerdmans, 1995), 58–59; Schreiner, *Romans*, 766–767.

[17] Romans 15:25–26, 31; 16:1, 15.

Earlier in this letter, the sanctifying work of the Spirit had also been highlighted in Romans 8:1-4. Christ came into the world so that those who believe in him would be able to truly obey the essence of the Law.[18] Central to Christ's death is the liberation of men and women from the death-dealing bondage of sin. This obedience and freedom is made a reality in believers by the Spirit, who is none other than the "Spirit of life," that is the Spirit of the living God, the source of all that is good. Thus, the liberating work of the Spirit is rooted in the saving work of Christ.[19]

Again in this chapter, Paul emphasizes that the Spirit's indwelling presence in the life of the believer provides him or her with rich resources to fight sin: Romans 8:12–14. Although the believer has been radically delivered from sin's tyranny, this does not mean—as so much of the teaching of the New Testament makes clear—that he or she now experientially enjoys perfect holiness. There is an ongoing battle with sin and thus the necessity of heeding the Apostle's admonition to mortify sin.[20]

This work of mortification—the "gradual annihilation of all the remainders of this cursed life of sin," as the Puritan author John Owen (1616–1683) aptly puts it[21]—involves the believer's complete involvement, though ultimately it is the Spirit's work. Owen well sums up the Apostle's thought in this regard when he states in his classic exposition of Romans 8:13, *The Mortification of Sin in Believers* (1656), that the Spirit:

> doth not so work our mortification in us as not to keep it still an act of our obedience. The Holy Ghost works in us

---

[18] Romans 8:4.

[19] Romans 8:2. See also Cranfield, *Romans*, 174; Fee, *God's Empowering Presence*, 519–538.

[20] Romans 8:13.

[21] *A Discourse Concerning the Holy Spirit* in *The Works of John Owen* (1850–1853 ed.; repr. London: The Banner of Truth Trust, 1965–1968), III, 545.

> and upon us, as we are fit to be wrought in and upon; that is, so as to preserve our own liberty and free obedience. He works upon our understandings, wills, consciences, and affections, agreeably to their own natures; he works in us and with us, not against us or without us; so that his assistance is an encouragement as to the facilitating of the work, and no occasion of neglect as to the work itself.[22]

In other words, this is a variation on one of the central ethical principles of the New Testament: be what you are. Because you are saints lead holy lives; live in holy conformity with the Spirit who indwells you. Since he is holy, be holy. Paul puts it this way at the close of another well-known passage that deals with the sanctifying work of the Spirit: "if we live by the Spirit, let us also walk by the Spirit."[23]

Sanctification, sexuality and the Spirit

Turning to Paul's first letter to the Thessalonians, we find that the recipients of this letter had once been men and women in bondage to idolatry.[24] That bondage, though, had been broken when, through Paul's preaching of the gospel, they had been freed by the power of the Holy Spirit.[25] Subsequently Paul had been forced to leave Thessalonica due to opposition to the gospel. Not surprisingly he was quite concerned to know how the Thessalonian believers were faring.[26] Cognizant of the pressure that pagan Graeco-Roman culture with its decadent sexual mores could exert upon those living within its midst, he reminded the Thessalonians

---

[22] *Of the Mortification of Sin in Believers* (*Works*, VI, 20). See also the comments of J.I. Packer, "'Keswick' and the Reformed Doctrine of Sanctification," *The Evangelical Quarterly* 27 (1955): 156.

[23] Galatians 5:25 ESV.

[24] 1 Thessalonians 1:9.

[25] 1 Thessalonians 1:5; 2:13.

[26] 1 Thessalonians 2:17; 3:5.

that central to God's will for their lives was their "sanctification."[27] Something of the importance that the Apostle places on this reminder is seen in the fact that he then proceeds to spell out what their sanctification entails.[28] Ever conscious of the authority which God has given to him as an Apostle,[29] Paul never hesitates to be specific in telling people what they should do and why.

For many Greeks or Romans of Paul's day there was nothing wrong with extra-marital sex as long as it was within the bounds of moderation. In this regard their culture was not too different from our contemporary world. But such a life-style was, and is, utterly opposed to the wishes of the Spirit. In Galatians 5:19, illicit forms of sex—spelled out as "sexual immorality (*porneia*), impurity (*akarthasia*), licentiousness (*aselgeia*)"—are placed among those things to which "the Spirit stands in…unrelieved opposition."[30] For Paul, full sexual expression is divinely designed by God to take place within the context of covenant marriage, where it is rooted in and surrounded by a framework of secure, intimate love.[31]

Sanctification also involves self-control,[32] though scholars are divided as to exactly what is the object of this self-control. Literally, the King James Version's rendition of the verse comes as close to a literal rendering as one could desire: "every one of you should know how to possess his vessel (*skeuos*) in sanctification and honour."[33] What exactly does Paul mean by the term "vessel"? *The Revised Standard Version*, following an interpretation

---

[27] 1 Thessalonians 4:3.

[28] 1 Thessalonians 4:4–8.

[29] See 1 Thessalonians 4:2. Cp. 1 Thessalonians 2:13.

[30] Fee, *God's Empowering Presence*, 441. The presence of *akarthasia* in 1 Thessalonians 4:7 indicates that Paul's concern is with sexual sin at this point. Thus Peterson, *Possessed by God*, 83.

[31] See Ephesians 5:25–33; 1 Corinthians 7:1–5.

[32] 1 Thessalonians 4:4.

[33] KJV.

that goes back to the Latin Father Augustine of Hippo (354–430) in the early fifth century, understands this phrase to be a euphemism for "wife." Thus, those who translated this version render this clause: "that each one of you know how to take a wife for himself in holiness and honor." The weight of evidence, however, is in favour of those who would translate the term *skeuos* as one's own body, a perspective that includes the early Christian author Tertullian (*fl.*190–215) and the French Reformer John Calvin (1509–1564).[34] Thus, for example, *The English Standard Version* has "each one of you know how to control his own body in holiness and honor."[35] Sanctification leads to self-control in sexual matters and a refusal to use one's own body—or that of another, which, if it is not in view in verse 4, is clearly in view in verse 6—as a "thing" simply to slake one's sexual thirst.

Paul now grounds these admonitions in three affirmations. First, there is the reality of God's judgment. One day God will judge all who have engaged in sexual immorality and die unrepentant.[36] Then, God's calling for all Christians is that they turn away from sexual "impurity" and lead lives marked by holiness.[37] Paul's third and final reason is that the professing believer who rejects—or "spurns" or "despises"—Paul's admonitions is not rejecting the words of a man. Not at all! Such a person is rejecting God himself. Now, Paul could very easily have stopped here. For a professing Christian to knowingly disobey God is serious enough. Why then does he go on to describe the God who is disobeyed as the giver of the Holy Spirit?

---

[34] Fee, *God's Empowering Presence*, 51–52, n.59. See also Peterson, *Possessed by God*, 83.

[35] See also the New International Version: "that each one of you should learn to control his own body in a way that is holy and honorable."

[36] 1 Thessalonians 4:6.

[37] 1 Thessalonians 4:7.

Two reasons are apparent. First of all, Paul lays particular stress on the Spirit as the *Holy* Spirit. The Greek literally runs thus: "God, who gives his Spirit, the Holy One, to you." Paul makes a point of highlighting this major characteristic of the Spirit: his holiness.[38] It's as if Paul was giving an answer to the question: "How do we know God desires our holiness?" Well, Paul replies, he's given us his *Holy* Spirit, the One who has the "power to make believers holy."[39] The Holy Spirit never comes into a human life apart from his holiness. The Holy Spirit "cannot come without His moral character," as George Verwer has rightly noted.[40]

Then, second, this gift of the Spirit is a fulfillment of the promise made by God in Ezekiel 36:27 and 37:14. Paul is clearly alluding to both of these verses when he says "God who gives his Holy Spirit to you."[41] At the heart of these verses from Ezekiel is the promise of a future gift of the Holy Spirit that will lead to genuine moral transformation. Paul is claiming that what God had promised to give in the days of Ezekiel has now been given and the reality of that inner transformation about which these Old Testament texts speak has been realized. Of course, this does not mean, as we have already noted, that the indwelling presence of the Spirit spells perfection. But as Gordon Fee notes, this "does mean that one is left without argument for helplessness" and "the pagan plea that man has no power to resist impure desires"

---

[38] Fee, *God's Empowering Presence*, 51, n.58.

[39] I. Howard Marshall, *1 and 2 Thessalonians* (Grand Rapids: Wm. B. Eerdmans/London: Marshall, Morgan & Scott Publ. Ltd., 1983), 114.

[40] *Revolution of Love and Balance* (1977 ed.; rev. Bromley, Kent/Waynesboro: STL Books, 1980), 19.

[41] Fee, *God's Empowering Presence*, 52; Peterson, *Possessed by God*, 84.

decisively answered.[42] To reject the command to be holy, then, is to say that one is not indwelt by the Spirit and not at all a believer.

The contemporary scene and the Spirit's ongoing power

The great contemporary challenge of embracing the biblical perspective about the holiness of the Triune God, in general, and the Spirit's sanctifying work, in particular, is that the ideas of human depravity *coram Deo* and therefore of the desperate need for the Spirit's sanctifying grace do not chime well with modern sensibilities. Men and women today do not view themselves as sinners who fall short of the holiness demanded by a thrice-holy God. Dominique Clift, writing in the late 1980s from the vantage point of twenty-five years of commenting on Canadian society and politics, well describes this modern situation when he writes:

> The most significant break with earlier religious attitudes, the one with the most far-reaching psychological consequences because of its effect on the way people see themselves, is the elimination of feelings of guilt and of unworthiness as the foundations of religious life. This development coincides with the appearance of more permissive social standards, particularly in sexual matters. … Somehow religion has moved beyond ethics: what has become uppermost today is the religious experience itself.[43]

J.I. Packer (1926–2020), in his own inimitable way, describes the same phenomenon as a day of "unwarrantably great thoughts of humanity and scandalously small thoughts of God." Our day, he

---

[42] Fee, *God's Empowering Presence*, 53. In the second quotation, Fee is quoting A. Plummer.

[43] *The Secret Kingdom: Interpretations of the Canadian Character* (Toronto: McClelland & Stewart, Inc., 1989), 205–206.

predicts, will be remembered as "the age of the God-shrinkers." The result, he says, is that:

> belief in God's sovereignty and omniscience, the majesty of his moral law and the terror of his judgments, the retributive consequences of the life we live here and the endlessness of eternity in which we will experience them, along with the intrinsic triunity of God and the divinity and personal return of Jesus Christ, is nowadays so eroded as to be hardly discernible. For many in our day, God is no more than a smudge.[44]

Part of the solution is to immerse ourselves afresh in the biblical perspectives about God and his holiness, and radically re-orient our mindset to what constitutes reality. Another part is to recognize that the Holy Spirit is still sovereign and has ways of overriding the barriers erected by erroneous thinking.

Consider the case of Mary Stewart, who, came to know Christ in that turbulent era of the late 1960s and early 1970s and found that she had some radical choices to make in her life. In her own words, she was:

> a very liberated young woman at the time. I had had a rich sexual fantasy life almost since I could remember. ... I had almost lost count of the number of men I had slept with in a serially monogamous fashion. I had taken advantage of the spirit of the Women's Movement (in which I was quite active) to begin exploring my own bisexuality. And I had no intention of giving any of that up. When I accepted Christ, I figured that it was the spirit of the law, not the letter, that mattered, that "love" was the overriding

---

[44] J.I. Packer, *A Passion for Holiness* (Wheaton: Crossway Books, 1992), 68–70, *passim.*

principle, and that I could witness in bed as easily as anywhere else.

But to my progressive astonishment, I found all that changing. Not quickly. Not all at once. Not by anyone's prying into my personal life or trying to send me on a guilt-trip (although I am sure I had lots of people praying for me). It was totally a process of God's working on me, one item of behaviour at a time, over many months, like patiently peeling one layer after another off an onion.[45]

As God's Spirit began to enable her to "walk in his statutes," as promised in Ezekiel 36:27,[46] she came to find herself "progressively liberated, gentled and strengthened" and that, in her own words, "I wanted God's Spirit more than I wanted transient physical titillation."[47]

Modern sensibilities be what they may, God's Spirit and his sweet grace are ultimately, thankfully, and blessedly irresistible. And this gives us great hope and encouragement. Well did John Ryland, Jr., the close friend of Andrew Fuller (1754–1815) and William Carey (1761–1834), express this truth, albeit with reference to a much broader context, in a 1792 circular letter that he drew up for the Calvinistic Baptist churches of the Northampton-shire Association:

> Surely the state both of the world, and of church, calls loudly upon us all to persist in wrestling instantly with God, for greater effusions of his Holy Spirit ... Let us not cease crying mightily unto the Lord, "until the Spirit be poured upon us from on high" [Isaiah 32:15]; then the wilderness shall become as a fruitful field, and the desert

---

[45] *Sexual Freedom* (Downers Grove: InterVarsity Press, 1974), 9–10.

[46] She actually cites this verse as part of the way God transformed her: *Sexual Freedom*, 9.

[47] *Sexual Freedom*, 16.

like the garden of God. Yes, beloved, the Scriptures cannot be broken. Jesus must reign universally. All nations shall own him. All people shall serve him. His kingdom shall be extended, not by human might, or power, but by the effusion of His Holy Spirit [cf. Zechariah 4:6].[48]

The Spirit's work will ultimately be victorious—both personally in those whom he indwells and globally.

---

[48] *Godly Zeal, Described and Recommended* (Circular Letter of the Northamptonshire Association; Nottingham, 1792), 1–2, 15.

4

"Rivers of dragons and mouths of lions and dark forces": The Holy Spirit & the struggle for holiness in Macarius[1]

In one of John Wesley's (1703–1791) most frequently preached sermons, "The Scripture-Way of Salvation," the Methodist leader sought to sum up the Wesleyan vision of the *ordo salutis* and correct misunderstandings of that rich vision. At one point Wesley was concerned to stress that in the overwhelming experience of conversion it was natural for those who go through

> such a change [to] imagine that all sin is gone! That it is utterly rooted out of their heart, and has no more any place therein! How easily do they draw that inference, "I *feel* no sin; therefore I *have* none." … But it is seldom long before they are undeceived, finding sin was only suspended, not destroyed. Temptations return and sin revives, showing that it was but stunned before, not dead. They now feel two principles in themselves, plainly contrary to each other: "the flesh lusting against the spirit," nature opposing the grace of God.[2]

---

[1] This paper was originally presented to the conference "Human and Christian Agency," which was an academic conference sponsored by the Society for Christian Psychology, September 17–18, 2010, at The Southern Baptist Theological Seminary, Louisville, Kentucky.

[2] John Wesley, *Sermons II, 34–70*, ed. Albert C. Outler (*The Works of John Wesley*, vol. 2; Nashville: Abingdon Press, 1985), 158–159.

Wesley then turned to a somewhat obscure fourth-century monastic author whom he called Macarius—known to modern scholars as either Pseudo-Macarius or Macarius-Symeon but whom this chapter will give the name by which he has gone for centuries, the one that Wesley gives him, namely, Macarius—to make the same point:

> How exactly did Macarius, fourteen hundred years ago, describe the present experience of the children of God! "The unskilful (or unexperienced), when grace operates, presently imagine they have no more sin. Whereas they that have discretion cannot deny that even we who have the grace of God may be molested again."[3]

Wesley was introduced to a German Pietist translation of Macarius' homilies in the colony of Georgia at the close of July, 1736, by some Moravian friends.[4] Wesley so appreciated these homilies that he would later edit and reprint some of them in the first volume of his *A Christian Library*, a collection of Christian literature designed for lay preachers.[5]

The major themes of the Macarian texts did indeed nicely dovetail with Wesley's interests, for in them Macarius especially set forth the biblical dimensions and theological implications of

---

[3] *Sermons II, 34–70*, ed. Outler, 159.

[4] John Wesley, *Journals and Diaries* I (1735–38), ed. W. Reginald Ward and Richard P. Heitzenrater (*The Works of John Wesley*, vol. 18; Nashville: Abingdon Press, 1988), 405–406.

[5] For reflection on Wesley's reading and use of Macarius, see Howard A. Snyder, "John Wesley and Macarius the Egyptian," *The Asbury Theological Journal* 45, no.2 (Fall 1990): 55–60, and especially Mark T. Kurowski, "The First Step Toward Grace: John Wesley's Use of the Spiritual Homilies of Macarius the Great," *Methodist History* 36, no.2 (January 1998): 113–124. For a general study of Wesley's reading of patristic literature, see Richard P. Heitzenrater, "John Wesley's Reading of and References to the Early Church Fathers" in S.T. Kimbrough, Jr., *Orthodox and Wesleyan Spirituality* (Crestwood: St Vladimir's Seminary Press, 2002), 25–32.

the salvific work of the Holy Spirit and explored the experience of the believer, who, though indwelt by the Spirit, nevertheless battles indwelling sin. In what follows, these major themes of Macarian theology and spirituality are explored as they are found primarily in one collection of Macarian texts, Collection II, the Fifty Spiritual Homilies, which have exercised a significant influence upon both Eastern and Western Christianity.

Who was Macarius?

While there is much that is unclear about Macarius, the author of these works, he appears to have been especially active between the 380s and the first decade of the fifth century.[6] He had strong ties to Syrian Christianity, although his mother tongue was most likely Greek. He would thus have been very comfortable with the theological ambience of Greek Christian life and piety.[7] His ministry seems to have been situated on the frontier of the Roman Empire in upper Syria and in southern Asia Minor, where he was the spiritual mentor of a number of monastic communities.[8]

Four collections of Macarius' homilies are extant.[9] In their *Rezeptionsgeschichte*, they have been historically linked to

---

[6] For major studies of Macarius' life and theology, see Hermann Dörries, *Die Theologie des Makarios-Symeon* (Göttingen: Vandenhoeck & Ruprecht, 1978); Columba Stewart, *"Working the Earth of the Heart": The Messalian Controversy in History, Texts, and Language to AD 431* (Oxford: Clarendon Press, 1991); Marcus Plested, *The Macarian Legacy: The Place of Macarius-Symeon in the Eastern Christian Tradition* (Oxford: Oxford University Press, 2004). See also the helpful studies by George A. Maloney, "Introduction" to his trans., *Pseudo-Macarius: The Fifty Spiritual Homilies and the Great Letter* (The Classics of Western Spirituality; New York/Mahwah: Paulist Press, 1992), 1–33 and Alexander Golitzin, "A Testimony to Christianity as Transfiguration: The Macarian Homilies and Orthodox Spirituality" in Kimbrough, ed., *Orthodox and Wesleyan Spirituality*, 129–156.

[7] Plested, *Macarian Legacy*, 14–15.

[8] Plested, *Macarian Legacy*, 15–16.

[9] For discussion of the four collections, see Stuart K. Burns, "Pseudo-Macarius and the Messalians: The Use of Time for the Common Good" in R.N. Swanson, ed., *The Use and Abuse of Time in Christian History* (Woodbridge: The Boydell Press for The Ecclesiastical History Society, 2002), 3, n.7; Plested, *Macarian Legacy*, 9–12.

Messalianism, an ascetic movement that was condemned at various councils, including the ecumenical Council of Ephesus in 431 as well as the earlier Synod of Side in Pamphylia (*c.*395), which was presided over by Amphilochius of Iconium, the protégé and close friend of Basil of Caesarea (*c.*330–379), one of the leading theologians of that era. According to those who condemned them, the Messalians argued that there was an indwelling demonic power in each human soul, and that only intense and ceaseless prayer could break the power that this demonic power held over the soul. Consequently, they were said to refuse to work so that they could devote their entire time to prayer. They were also said to affirm physical experiences of the Spirit, made light of the sacraments of the church as well as the ministry of those in official positions of power.[10] Although there are a number of clear points of contact between the Messalians and Macarius, especially with regard to Macarius' deep interest in the Spirit, the burden of current scholarly opinion is that Macarius cannot be regarded as a Messalian.[11]

---

[10] Stewart, *"Working the Earth of the Heart,"* 52–69, *passim*; Maloney, "Introduction," 8–9; David Roach, "Macarius the Augustinian: Grace and Salvation in the Spiritual Homilies of Macarius-Symeon," *Eusebeia* 8 (Fall 2007): 77–78. In the words of Robert Murray, the Messalians "laid too much stress on experience of the Spirit for the liking of ecclesiastics in the institutional Church" (*Symbols of Church and Kingdom. A Study in Early Syriac Tradition* [Cambridge: Cambridge University Press, 1975], 35).

On the question of the relationship of Macarius to the Messalians, see, in addition to the monographs cited in note 5, John Meyendorff, "Messalianism or Anti-Messalianism? A Fresh Look at the «Macarian» Problem" in Patrick Granfield and Josef A. Jungmann, eds., *Kyriakon: Festschrift Johannes Quasten* (Münster: Verlag Aschendorff, 1970), II, 585–590; Reinhart Staats, "Messalianism and AntiMessalianism in Gregory of Nyssa's De Virignitate," *The Patristic and Byzantine Review* 2 (1983): 27–44; Stuart K. Burns, "Charisma and spirituality in the early Church: A study of Messalianism and Pseudo-Macarius" (PhD thesis, University of Leeds, 1990); and Alexander Golitzin, "Temple and Throne of the Divine Glory: 'Pseudo-Macarius' and Purity of Heart, Together with Some Remarks on the Limitations and Usefulness of Scholarship" in Harriet A. Luckman and Linda Kulzer, eds., *Purity of Heart in Early Ascetic and Monastic Literature. Essays in Honor of Juana Raasch, O.S.B.* (Collegeville: Liturgical Press, 1999), 107–117.

[11] See, for example, Stewart, *"Working the Earth of the Heart"* and Burns, "Pseudo-Macarius and the Messalians," 1–12.

Confirmation of this perspective of recent Macarian scholarship is found in Macarius' strong connections to the Cappadocian theologians, in particular, Basil and his brother Gregory of Nyssa.[12] For example, in Nyssen's *In suam ordinationem* (*On his ordination*), preached at the induction of his friend Gregory of Nazianzus (*c.*330–389/90) as bishop of Constantinople, he mentions various ascetics at the ordination—whom Reinhart Staats plausibly believes to have been Macarius and some of his followers. Gregory has a deep admiration for these men, who have, he says,

> like Abraham left their own country, their family and the world at large. They look to heaven; they cut themselves off, so to say, from human life; they are superior to the passions of nature ... They do not struggle with words, they do not study rhetoric; but they have such power over the spirits that they expel demons not through syllogistic arts but through the power of faith.[13]

This deep admiration for Macarius on the part of Nyssen as well as Macarius' concern that he shared with the Cappadocians to defend the deity of the Spirit were key factors that helped preserve his writings.[14]

---

[12] See Plested, *Macarian Legacy*, 46–58, *passim*.

[13] Cited Plested, *Macarian Legacy*, 54. See Reinhart Staats, "Die Basilianische Verherrlichung des Heiligen Geistes auf dem Konzil zu Konstantinopel 381. Ein Beitrag zum Ursprung der Formel 'Kerygma und Dogma,'" *Kerygma und Dogma* 25 (1979): 232–253. This is not to say that Gregory did not have some distinct concerns about some of Macarius' views. See Staats, "Messalianism and AntiMessalianism in Gregory of Nyssa's De Virignitate," *passim*.

[14] Plested, *Macarian Legacy*, 57–58.

The tragedy of the Fall[15]

The awful devastation caused by the fall of Adam and the experiential reality of the tyranny of sin that ensued for his progeny as a result of his disobedience regularly impressed themselves upon the mind of Macarius.[16] Prior to the fall, Adam was clothed with the glory of the Holy Spirit,[17] and thus knew the Spirit's personal instruction as well as that of the Word of God—the "Word was everything to him."[18] He lived in total purity, was pleasing to God in all areas of his life and he had sovereign control over his thoughts and actions.[19] When he disobeyed God's Word of his own free will, though, his disobedience became the doorway through which all kinds of evil were sowed in the world, as well as being the vehicle for the entrance of "tumult, confusion, and battle" into the inner being of men and women.[20] After the fall, Adam and his descendants lost both God and their God-given beauty. God, ever "the Lover of mankind," wept over his fallen creation,[21] for they were now marred by corruption, spiritual ugliness,

---

[15] I have used Maloney's translation in what follows since it is most readily available. The other major English translation of Collection II is A.J. Mason, *Fifty Spiritual Homilies of St. Macarius the Egyptian* (London: Society for Promoting Christian Knowledge, 1921). When reference is made to the Greek in the text, then the relevant column and section in J.P. Migne, ed., *Patrologiae cursus completes...series Graeca* (Paris, 1860), 34:449–822, henceforth abbreviated as PG 34, is given in brackets after the citation of the primary source.

I have also made very occasional use of the seven untranslated homilies published by G.L. Marriott: *Macarii Anecdota: Seven Unpublished Homilies of Macarius* (Harvard Theological Studies, vol. 5; Cambridge: Harvard University Press, 1918). Following the numbering of Plested (*Macarian Legacy*, 10 and n.5), these are Homilies 51–57. Where they are used I have designated the reference by the name of Marriott with the appropriate page in brackets.

[16] See Plested, *Macarian Legacy*, 35–36 and Roach, "Macarius the Augustinian," 78–79, for an overview of Macarius' thinking about the impact of the fall.

[17] *Homily* 5.11, 12; 12.6–8; 20.1.

[18] *Homily* 12.6–8 (Maloney, *Fifty Spiritual Homilies*, 99–100).

[19] *Homily* 12.7–8; 15.25.

[20] *Homily* 15.49. See also *Homily* 1.7.

[21] *Homily* 4.16; 30.7; 46.3.

and "a great stench" that emanated from their souls.[22] Fallen men and women were now, in one of Macarius' most trenchant descriptions, like "houses of prostitution and ill-fame in which all sorts of immoral debaucheries go on."[23] Dominating their lives was a love of this age and its passions and concerns.[24] Instead of their Maker being their Lord, Satan himself became their prince and ruler, and filled their hearts with spiritual darkness.[25]

Ever true to his nature as a wicked tyrant, Satan did not spare any area of human existence from his deadly touch and control. The "evil prince corrupted" the human frame "completely, not sparing any of its members from its slavery, not its thoughts, neither the mind nor the body."[26] When men and women act under the impulse of these evils, they think that they are doing so on the basis of their "own determination." But the reality is they are controlled by the power of sin.[27] From Macarius' vantage-point, every fallen human being is so under sin's dominion that he or she can "no longer see freely but sees evilly, hears evilly, and has swift feet to perpetrate evil acts."[28]

Although this extremely realistic view of the Fall and its impact would appear to commit Macarius to a strongly determinist perspective with regard to the human condition, Macarius vehemently maintained that men and women ultimately commit evil of their own free will. As he asserted on one occasion: "Our nature … is capable of both good and evil, either of divine grace or of the opposing power, but never through compulsion."[29] However, this

---

[22] *Homily* 30.7–8. See also *Homily* 24.4.

[23] *Homily* 12.2.

[24] *Homily* 21.2; 24.2.

[25] *Homily* 5.2; 21.2.

[26] *Homily* 2.1 (Maloney, *Fifty Spiritual Homilies*, 44). See also *Homily* 16.6.

[27] *Homily* 15.49.

[28] *Homily* 2.2 (Maloney, *Fifty Spiritual Homilies*, 45).

[29] *Homily* 15.25 (PG34.592D). Author's translation.

ability to choose appears to extend solely to individual sinful acts.[30] What human beings cannot do is remove the deeply-rooted interiority of sin itself. Its dominion within the human heart is far too strong to be defeated by human energy alone.[31] It is "impossible," Macarius stated on one occasion, "to separate the soul from sin unless God should calm and turn back this evil wind, inhabiting both the soul and body."[32] Again, as he put it elsewhere: "without the Lord Jesus and the working of divine power," that is, the Holy Spirit, "no one can ... be a Christian."[33]

"The sweetness of the Spirit"[34]

This situation can only be changed for the better, in Macarius' thinking, through a person persistently crying out to God for help to transform him or her from "bitterness to sweetness."[35] So it is that Macarius can argue that "even the man confirmed in evil, or the one completely immersed in sin and making himself a vessel of the devil ... still has freedom to become a chosen vessel."[36] Given Macarius' views about the devastation that has resulted from the Fall, some of which has been detailed above, this statement must be taken to mean that Macarius believes human beings have enough freedom to cry out to God for salvation.[37]

---

[30] Mariette Canévet, "Macaire" in A. Rayez, A. Derville, and A. Solignac, *Dictionnaire de spiritualité* (Paris: Beauchesne, 1980), X, 31–32; Golitzin, "A Testimony to Christianity as Transfiguration," 132.

[31] *Homily* 3.4; 27.22; Stewart, *"Working the Earth of the Heart,"* 74; Golitzin, "Temple and Throne of the Divine Glory," 124–125.

[32] *Homily* 2.3 (Maloney, *Fifty Spiritual Homilies*, 45). See also *Homily* 3.4.

[33] *Homily* 17.10 (Maloney, *Fifty Spiritual Homilies*, 139).

[34] *Homily* 47.15 (Maloney, *Fifty Spiritual Homilies*, 238, altered).

[35] *Homily* 2.3; 4.4, 8; 18.2; 20.1; 31.1; 44.9; 47.7, 10. The quote is from *Homily* 31.1 (PG 34.728D; Maloney, *Fifty Spiritual Homilies*, 194, altered). See also Golitzin, "A Testimony to Christianity as Transfiguration," 132.

[36] *Homily* 15.40 (PG34.604A; Maloney, *Fifty Spiritual Homilies*, 123, altered).

[37] *Homily* 46.3.

Without God's aid through the gift of the Spirit no one will ever "return to their senses from their intoxication with the material realm."[38] Without the life-giving power of the Spirit, one is dead "as far as the kingdom goes, being unable to do any of the things of God," for "the Spirit is the life of the soul."[39] And so great is the plague of sin in the human heart, healing is only found through the medicine of the Holy Spirit.[40]

Macarius also likens the conversion of a person to the taming of a horse. Prior to being tamed, an unconverted person is like a "wild and indomitable" horse. But once "he hears the Word of God and believes, he is bridled by the Spirit. He puts away his wild habits and carnal thoughts, being now guided by Christ, his rider."[41] The Apostle Paul was, for Macarius, a prime example of such conversion. He had been living under the "tyrannical spirit of sin," and as a persecutor of the Church he can be rightly described as being "steeped in evil and turned back to a wild state." But Christ arrested his progress in sin, and "flooding him with ineffable light," liberated him from sin's domination. Here, Macarius stated, we see Christ's "goodness ... and his power to change."[42] From another angle, the Spirit comes into the entirety of a person's being to put it in order and beautify it just as "a house that has its master at home shows forth an abundance of orderliness, and beauty and harmony."[43]

This gift of the Spirit in conversion, though, is only the beginning of what formed a major aspect of Macarius' theological reflections, namely, the remarkable nature of life in the Spirit.

---

[38] *Homily* 24.5 (PG 34.665B–C). Author's translation.

[39] *Homily* 30.3, 6 (Maloney, *Fifty Spiritual Homilies*, 191, 192).

[40] *Homily* 20.7 (PG34.653A). Author's translation.

[41] *Homily* 23.2 (Maloney, *Fifty Spiritual Homilies*, 156).

[42] *Homily* 44.8 (Maloney, *Fifty Spiritual Homilies*, 225–226).

[43] *Homily* 11.3; 33.3 (Maloney, *Fifty Spiritual Homilies*, 202). See also *Homily* 5.9; 27.19.

Sometimes the believer's life is flooded with the joy of the Spirit and he is like "a spouse who enjoys conjugal union with her bridegroom."[44] On other occasions, he finds himself overwhelmed by grief as he prays in accordance with the "love of the Spirit towards mankind."[45] Other times there is "a burning of the Spirit" which enflames the heart with regard to the things of God.[46] Then, just as "deep, conjugal love" between man and a woman lead them to marry and leave father and mother and all other earthly loves, so "true fellowship with the Holy Spirit, the heavenly and loving Spirit" ultimately brings freedom from the loves of this age.[47]

It bears noting that the gift of the Spirit is dependent on the cross-work of Christ. Likening the cross to the work of a gardener, Macarius argued that through the cross Christ, "the heavenly and true gardener," removed from the barren soul "the thorns and thistles of evil spirits" as well as uprooting and burning with fire "the weeds of sin." With the removal of these, he can now plant in the soul "the most beautiful paradise of the Spirit."[48] The gift of the Spirit is a fruit of the death of Christ.

Macarius thinks about the cross in primarily two ways.[49] On the one hand, the cross is a place of healing and Christ is "the true physician" who has come to heal "everyone afflicted by the incurable wound of sin."[50] Then, the cross is conceived of as a place of ransom, where Christ's life is given in payment for those of sinners. Thus, Macarius argued that Christ's blood was poured out

---

[44] *Homily* 18.7.

[45] *Homily* 18.8 (Maloney, *Fifty Spiritual Homilies*, 144).

[46] *Homily* 25.9 (Maloney, *Fifty Spiritual Homilies*, 163).

[47] *Homily* 4.15 (Maloney, *Fifty Spiritual Homilies*, 56–57, altered).

[48] *Homily* 28.4 (Maloney, *Fifty Spiritual Homilies*, 185, altered).

[49] For Macarius' thinking about the cross, see especially Christine Mengus, "Le «cœur» dans les «Cinquante Homélies spirituelles» du Pseudo-Macaire (III)," *Collectanea Cisterciensia* 59 (1997): 124–126; Roach, "Macarius the Augustinian," 80–81.

[50] *Homily* 20.4–8. The quotes are from *Homily* 20.6 (PG 34.653A) and 20.4 respectively.

on the cross so that there would be "life and deliverance for humanity."[51] Again, he could state that Christ came to earth to "suffer on behalf of all and to buy them back with his blood."[52]

"Rivers of dragons and mouths of lions and dark forces"[53]

The gift of the indwelling Spirit, though, does not mean that the one whom he indwells is now exempt from spiritual warfare, for, "where the Holy Spirit is, there follows … persecution and struggle."[54] As Marcus Plested has noted, Macarius argued for "a profoundly militant Christianity."[55] There is persecution of the Church by the powers of this age.[56] The faithful believer is "nailed to the cross of Christ" and knows what it is to experience "the stigmata and wounds of the Lord."[57] And there is struggle within the heart of the Christian, such that even the most mature Christian can fall back into a life of sin.[58] In part, Macarius argued, this is because of the malice of Satan, who is "without mercy and hates humans," and thus never hesitates to attack Christians.[59] In part, though, it is because Christians, even "those who are intoxicated with God" and "bound by the Holy Spirit," are not under constraint to do that which pleases God, for they still have their free

---

[51] *Homily* 47.8 (Maloney, *Fifty Spiritual Homilies*, 235).

[52] *Homily* 24.3 (Maloney, *Fifty Spiritual Homilies*, 158). See especially *Homily* 11.9–15 for Macarius' most detailed development of the cross as a place of ransom.

[53] *Homily* 16.13 (Maloney, *Fifty Spiritual Homilies*, 134). For this expression, see also *Homily* 15.50; 43.3.

[54] *Homily* 15.12 (Maloney, *Fifty Spiritual Homilies*, 112).

[55] *Macarian Legacy*, 37. For discussion of this theme, see Plested, *Macarian Legacy*, 36–38; Christine Mengus, "Le «cœur» dans les «Cinquante Homélies spirituelles» du Pseudo-Macaire (II)," *Collectanea Cisterciensia* 59 (1997), 36–38; Golitzin, "Temple and Throne of the Divine Glory," 125.

[56] *Homily* 15.12. See also *Homily* 9.2–7.

[57] *Homily* 10.1 (PG34.541A); 53.17 (Marriott, 36; author's translation). See also *Homily* 12.5.

[58] *Homily* 8.5; 15.4, 14, 16, 36; 26.17.

[59] *Homily* 15.18 (Maloney, *Fifty Spiritual Homilies*, 114).

will.[60] Thus Macarius read Ephesians 4:30 to mean that it was up to Christians' "will and freedom of choice to honour the Holy Spirit and not to grieve him" through sin.[61]

Macarius personally knew men who seemed to be making great progress in the Christian life and then, through yielding to sin, lost everything. One man, who was a Roman aristocrat, seeking to follow Christ, sold his possessions and freed all of his slaves. He soon gained a reputation for being a holy man. Pride entered in and eventually he "fell completely into debaucheries and a thousand evils."[62] Yet another suffered as a confessor in what was probably the last great imperial Roman persecution of the Church, namely, that of Diocletian. He was horribly tortured. While in prison, a Christian woman sought to minister to him, but tempted by sexual lust, they "fell into fornication."[63] The Christian experience of life in the Spirit in this world was thus one of great struggle against evil powers, whom, in a memorable turn of phrase, Macarius likened to "rivers of dragons and mouths of lions and dark forces."[64]

Ultimately, though, it is not the human will that is the determinant factor in perseverance. It is "the power of the divine Spirit" that is the critical necessity for a person to attain to eternal life. True to the pneumatological emphasis of his thought, Macarius thus concluded: "if [a person] thinks he can effect a perfect work by himself without the help of the Spirit, he is totally in error. Such an attitude is unbecoming one who strives for heavenly places, for the kingdom."[65]

---

[60] *Homily* 15.40 (PG34.604B). Author's translation. The phrase "bound by the Spirit" is taken from Paul's statement in Acts 20:22. See also *Homily* 15.36; 27.10–11.

[61] *Homily* 27.9 (Maloney, *Fifty Spiritual Homilies*, 178).

[62] *Homily* 27.14 (Maloney, *Fifty Spiritual Homilies*, 180).

[63] *Homily* 27.15 (Maloney, *Fifty Spiritual Homilies*, 180).

[64] *Homily* 16.13 (Maloney, *Fifty Spiritual Homilies*, 134).

[65] *Homily* 24.3, 5 (Maloney, *Fifty Spiritual Homilies*, 158).

A concluding word

Macarius' vision of the Christian life then is one of victorious liberation from the tyranny of sin by the power of the Spirit of Christ.[66] It begins with a heart dominated by evil, due to Adam's disobedience. Conversion brings liberty from this dreadful state of affairs, but plunges the believer into a warfare with indwelling sin and external spiritual enemies. Although the human will is now truly free to follow Christ or go back into a life of sin, ultimately it is the grace of the Spirit that spells victory in this war.

In many ways, Macarius' homilies are not marked by the deep theological sophistication of his contemporary Gregory of Nyssa, whom he influenced and who, like Macarius, was deeply interested in the twin themes of theological anthropology and pneumatology. Nevertheless, Macarius' deeply realistic approach to the human condition, his emphasis on the vital necessity of the Holy Spirit to effect eternal transformation, and his desire to take seriously human responsibility reveal him to be a thinker worthy of attention in our day that is also marked by a fascination with spirituality and a passionate interest in what it means to be truly human.

---

[66] Plested, *Macarian Legacy*, 78–79.

5

Word and Spirit:
Apollos and Hilary of Poitiers as
models for spiritual advance[1]

Ministers lift up their voice, and God makes bare his arm;
ministers persuade, and God enables, nay, constrains, men to comply.
… Ministers stand at the door and knock; the Spirit comes with his key, and opens the door.

Benjamin Beddome (1717–1795)

In the early days of the Reformation in Germany, Martin Luther (1483–1546) reflected on why the Reformation truths that he and his colleagues were preaching and publishing were making such a deep impact on various parts of German-speaking Europe. To the God-centered Luther, the answer was patent:

> I simply taught, preached, and wrote God's Word; other-wise I did nothing. And while I slept or drank Wittenberg beer with my friends …, the Word so greatly weakened the papacy that no prince or emperor ever inflicted such losses upon it. I did nothing; the Word did everything.[2]

In emphasizing that the "Word did everything," Luther is not simply giving his own personal opinion, but making plain a vital theme in the history of the Christian faith. In times of spiritual

---

[1] The heart of this chapter was given as an address at the End of Year Service at London Theological Seminary, London, England, June 14, 2008.

[2] *The Second Invocavit Sermon* in Ronald J. Sider, ed., *Karlstadt's Battle with Luther: Documents in a Liberal-Radical Debate* (Philadelphia: Fortress Press, 1978), 24.

69

advance, the Church is borne along by the Word of God as it lays bare the secrets of human hearts and brings sinners to conversion.[3] Speaking of this pattern in the history of the Church, Iain Murray put it this way: "The advance of the church is ever preceded by a recovery of preaching [the Word]."[4]

Now, in the Scriptures there is one book that especially emphasizes this theme of the power of the Word of God in the advance of the Church, the Book of Acts. And it does so by linking this advance to the invincible work of the Holy Spirit who empowers the Word. Before we look at the way Luke has constructed the Book of Acts around this theme, a few introductory remarks about Acts are necessary.

The purpose of Acts

Acts, as is well known, is the second part of a two-volume work—the first volume being the Gospel of Luke[5]—in which the origins of Christianity are traced back to the life and ministry of Christ and the way in which Christianity moved out from its Palestinian origins to become a movement of God's Holy Spirit detailed. It is clear that Luke believed that the recounting of this history has value and significance, and that it can be a means of encouraging God's people and confirming their faith.[6] For him, church history is anything but a dry, dusty subject. Rather, we remember the history of God's Church because in that realm we have an exciting and fascinating window in which to see God at work powerfully by

---

[3] See Hebrews 4:12–13; James 1:18.

[4] "Lloyd-Jones: Messenger of Grace," *The Banner of Truth* 536 (May 2008): 32.

[5] See Luke 1:1–4 and Acts 1:1.

[6] F.F. Bruce, *The Acts of the Apostles* (3rd. ed.; Grand Rapids: Wm. B. Eerdmans/Leicester: Apollos, 1990), 22; I. Howard Marshall, *The Acts of the Apostles* (Leicester, England: InterVarsity Press/Grand Rapids: Wm. B. Eerdmans, 1980), 49. This reading of Luke 1:1–4 by the way assumes that Theophilus was a believer (Marshall, *Acts of the Apostles*, 21,

his Spirit bringing glory to his Son. In the quaint words of New England Puritanism, Luke was thus one of the "Lord's remembrancers."

Now, Acts also has a more specific purpose, and that purpose can be seen in what many have considered as the theme verse of the entire Book of Acts, namely, Acts 1:8, "you will receive power when the Holy Spirit has come upon you, and you will be my witnesses in Jerusalem and in all Judea and Samaria, and to the end of the earth."[7] Here we see the three major threads that run through the Book of Acts:

- First, the advance of the church is impossible, utterly impossible, without the presence and power of the Holy Spirit. Without him, nothing of any lasting value could have been achieved. Jesus' words about himself in John 15:5 are very appropriate in this regard. "Without me," he said in that text, "you can do nothing." Just as truly, we can state that the Book of Acts teaches: "Without the Holy Spirit, we can do nothing."[8]
- Second, the Spirit is pleased to use the witness of the Apostles, i.e. their preaching and sharing of the gospel, the Word of God, to advance the rule of Christ.
- Third, this advance encompasses not only Jew but also Gentile—the church's mission is to the "end of the earth," to the whole of the inhabited globe.[9]

---

[7] ESV.

[8] See F.W. Dillistone, "The Holy Spirit and Christian Mission" in Gerald H. Anderson, ed., *The Theology of the Christian Mission* (New York: McGraw-Hill Book Co., Inc., 1961), 273; James Dunn, *Baptism in the Holy Spirit. A Re-examination of the New Testament Teaching on the Gift of the Spirit in relation to Pentecostalism today* (London: SCM Press, 1970), 49.

[9] Brian S. Rosner, "The Progress of the Word" in I. Howard Marshall and David Peterson, eds., *Witness to the Gospel. The Theology of Acts* (Grand Rapids/Cambridge: Wm. B. Eerdmans, 1998), 218.

Of these three themes, it is the second one—the Word as the means of the Spirit's advance of the rule of Christ—that is probably the most central to Luke's purpose in writing his history of the Apostolic Church. Led by the Spirit, Luke has divided Acts into six panels in which this theme is emphasized again and again by means of summary statements that conclude the six panels. Read these summary statements and notice the theme of the victorious advance of the Word:

- "And the word of God continued to increase, and the number of the disciples multiplied greatly in Jerusalem, and a great many of the priests became obedient to the faith" (Acts 6:7 ESV).
- "So the church throughout all Judea and Galilee and Samaria had peace and was being built up. And walking in the fear of the Lord and in the comfort of the Holy Spirit, it multiplied" (Acts 9:31 ESV).
- "But the word of God increased and multiplied" (Acts 12:24 ESV).
- "So the churches were strengthened in the faith, and they increased in numbers daily" (Acts 16:5 ESV).
- "So the word of the Lord continued to increase and prevail mightily" (Acts 19:20 ESV).
- "He [i.e. Paul] lived there [i.e. Rome] two whole years at his own expense, and welcomed all who came to him, proclaiming the kingdom of God and teaching about the Lord Jesus Christ with all boldness and without hindrance" (Acts 28:30–31 ESV).

The emphasis of these summary statements is that the Spirit so empowered the preaching and witness of the Word of God during the Apostolic era that it was unstoppable or, as Luke puts it in the very last word of his book—a very elegant adverb—Paul's preaching went forth "without hindrance" (*akōlytōs*).

Now, an excellent illustration of this theme is found in Luke's vignette about the Alexandrian Jewish preacher Apollos in Acts 18:24–28.

Apollos—"aglow with the Spirit"

As James D.G. Dunn has noted, "Apollos is one of the most intriguing figures in earliest Christian history." One of the main reasons for this, Dunn goes on to note, is Apollos' link with Alexandria, which, along with Rome, Corinth, and Syrian Antioch, was one of the four most important cities in the Roman Imperium.[10] It was a key centre of learning, especially Jewish learning and literature, and was later a major locale for early Christian theology.[11] It is noteworthy that Luke does not tell us how Christianity came to Alexandria,[12] though he does give us this fascinating glimpse of one of the earliest of Alexandrian believers.

Apollos—a short form for the longer name Apollonius[13]—is described as a Jew, an "eloquent man" or one who was well-educated.[14] We are also told that he was "competent"—or mighty (*dynatos*)—"in the Scriptures," that is, a man who knew how to

---

[10] Joseph A. Fitzmeyer, *The Acts of the Apostles* (*The Anchor Bible*; New York: Doubleday, 1998), 638.

[11] *The Acts of the Apostles* (Valley Forge: Trinity Press International, 1996), 249.

[12] For some brief reflections on the beginnings of Alexandrian Christianity, see F.F. Bruce, *Men and Movements in the Primitive Church. Studies in Early Non-Pauline Christianity* (Exeter: Paternoster Press, 1979), 71–76.

[13] Colin J. Hemer, *The Book of Acts in the Setting of Hellenistic History*, ed. Conrad H. Gempf (Tübingen: J.C.B. Mohr [Paul Siebeck], 1989), 206, 233.

[14] Acts 18:24. See also Bruce, *Men and Movements*, 68; C.K. Barrett, *The Acts of the Apostles* (Edinburgh: T & T Clark, 1998), II, 887; Ben Witherington, III, *The Acts of the Apostles. A Socio-Rhetorical Commentary* (Grand Rapids/Cambridge: Wm. B. Eerdmans/Carlisle: Paternoster Press, 1998), 564; Darrell L. Bock, *Acts* (Baker Exegetical Commentary on the New Testament; Grand Rapids: Baker, 2007), 591.

interpret and apply the Old Testament with some skill.[15] It was due to this description of Apollos' abilities that Martin Luther suggested that he was the author of Hebrews. It appears that Luther was the first to make such a proposal, but it is a view that has not won a substantial following for the very reason that we have no clearly identified writing of Apollos to compare with Hebrews.[16]

Apollos also had been given instruction about "the way of the Lord"—a phrase that Luke regularly uses to designate Christianity[17]—and he spoke and "taught accurately (*akribōs*) the things concerning Jesus."[18] Here it is vital to recall that in the final summary statement of the Book of Acts, found in Acts 28:30–31, we are told that Paul was in Rome "teaching the things concerning the Lord Jesus Christ."[19] Just as Paul is an accurate Christian teacher, so it seems is Apollos.[20]

Sandwiched between these two statements in verse 25 is Luke's remark that Apollos was "fervent in"—literally, "boiling with" or "aglow with"—"the Spirit." Some Bible scholars have taken this to be a reference to Apollos' human spirit.[21] But coming as it does between the statements noted above, this description is best read as a statement about the Holy Spirit. Apollos was aglow

---

[15] Acts 18:24. See W. Hulitt Gloer, "Apollos" in Watson E. Mills, ed., *The Lutterworth Dictionary of the Bible* (Cambridge: Lutterworth Press, [1994]), 46.

[16] Bruce, *Men and Movements*, 79–84, *passim*; L.D. Hurst, "Apollos" in David Noel Freedman *et al.*, eds., *The Anchor Bible Dictionary* (New York: Doubleday, 1992), 1:301; Gloer, "Apollos," 46.

[17] See Acts 9:2; 19:9, 23; 22:4; 24:14, 22. Also see C.K. Barrett, *The Acts of the Apostles. A Shorter Commentary* (London/New York: T & T Clark, 2002), 285.

[18] Acts 18:25.

[19] ASV.

[20] Barrett, *Acts of the Apostles*, II, 888.

[21] See William J. Larkin Jr., *Acts* (Downers Grove/Leicester: InterVarsity Press, 1995), 270–271; Bock, *Acts*, 591–592.

with the Holy Spirit.[22] In other words, there seems to be little doubt that Luke presents Apollos as a Christian believer.[23]

Apollos and Paul: co-workers

There was an area of deficiency, though. When Priscilla and Aquila hear Apollos teaching powerfully in the synagogue at Ephesus they perceive a problem. They rectify the problem by meeting with Apollos privately and explaining "the way of God more accurately."[24] What was the problem? It is noteworthy that Luke does not spell out at all what Priscilla and Aquila told Apollos. It may well have had to do with Christian baptism, since Luke does tell us "he knew only the baptism of John."[25] But nothing is said about Apollos receiving Christian baptism. What is critical for Luke is that Apollos listened to Priscilla and Aquila and was strengthened by their private instruction.[26]

Why is this event important to Luke? Well, Acts 13–28 are primarily about the mission of Paul and his apostolic band. Here in Acts 18, right in the middle of Luke's long history of the Pauline mission, we read of a different mission headed up by Apollos. After being taught by Priscilla and Aquila—who are within the Pauline mission circle[27]—Apollos crossed over to Achaia and Corinth,

---

[22] See the same phrase in Romans 12:11. Also see John Calvin, *The Acts of the Apostles 14–28*, trans. John W. Fraser (Edinburgh: Saint Andrews Press, 1966), 144: "Luke attributes his [that is, Apollos'] fervor to the Spirit;" John B. Polhill, *Acts* (*The New American Commentary*, vol. 26; Nashville: Broadman Press, 1992), 396; Dunn, *Acts of the Apostles*, 250; Witherington, *Acts of the Apostles*, 565; Max Turner, *Power from on High: The Spirit in Israel's Restoration and Witness in Luke-Acts* (*Journal of Pentecostal Theology Supplement Series*, vol. 9; Sheffield: Sheffield Academic Press, 2000), 389 and nn.124–125.

[23] See the discussion by Witherington, *Acts of the Apostles*, 564–566.

[24] Acts 18:26.

[25] Acts 18:25. See Polhill, *Acts*, 396–397.

[26] Thus Beverly Roberts Gaventa, *The Acts of the Apostles* (*Abingdon New Testament Commentaries*; Nashville: Abingdon Press, 2003), 265.

[27] See Acts 18:1–3; 1 Corinthians 16:19; Romans 16:3–5; 2 Timothy 4:19.

with the blessing of the brothers at Ephesus.[28] Apollos' ministry there was a highly successful one, for, Luke tells us, he edified the believers and powerfully refuted those Jews who argued against the Christian claims about Christ.[29] After he had left, though, some believers, deeply impressed with Apollos, used the differences between Paul and Apollos to criticize Paul. Some went so far as to label themselves followers of Apollos. Others disagreed—Paul was their man.[30]

One answer to this schism was Paul's response in 1 Corinthians 1–3: "I planted, Apollos watered, but God gave the growth. So neither he who plants nor he who waters is anything, but only God who gives the growth"[31] In Paul's mind, he and Apollos are co-workers (*synergoi*);[32] he clearly regards Apollos as a trusted brother and fellow teacher.[33] In the words of F.F. Bruce, their relationship was one of "mutual esteem and indeed affection."[34] But ultimately it is not they, but God who builds the Church, and so dividing over who might be the better preacher is simply wrong. A second answer is here in Acts 18. Luke is reminding the reader that Paul and Apollos were ultimately engaged in the same mission.[35]

Beyond these passages in Acts and 1 Corinthians—assuming Apollos was not the author of Hebrews—we know virtually nothing more about the Alexandrian preacher.[36] In the words of F.F.

---

[28] Acts 18:27.

[29] Acts 18:27–28.

[30] 1 Corinthians 1:10–13; 3:1–23. See Bruce, *Men and Movements*, 68–69.

[31] 1 Corinthians 3:6–7 ESV.

[32] 1 Corinthians 3:9.

[33] See 1 Corinthians 16:12; Titus 3:13. Paul's confidence in their friendship is seen also in the free use he makes of the names sof Apollos and himself in his response to the Corinthians. He is more guarded in his use of Peter's name. See Bruce, *Men and Movements*, 65–66. See also Polhill, *Acts*, 398, n.11; Witherington, *Acts of the Apostles*, 568–569.

[34] Bruce, *Men and Movements*, 69.

[35] See Dunn, *Acts of the Apostles*, 249.

[36] Do note Titus 3:13, though.

Bruce, "for a brief space" Apollos "traverses the Pauline circle and endears himself to its members and their leader, makes a powerful impression on fellow-Jews and fellow-Christians in Ephesus and Corinth, and then vanishes from our sight"[37]—though, thankfully not from the Lord's sight, who will remember all that Apollos did for Christ on that great Day when he comes again.

The Spirit's use of the Word in the Ancient Church
Within the larger purpose of Acts, though, there is one more thing that the "Lord's Remembrancer," Luke, wants us to remember about Apollos' life as a minister of the gospel. His life perfectly illustrates the great theme of Acts that we have noted above: through Christ-centered preaching of the Word of God the rule of Christ was advanced into the world of the Roman Empire.[38] Apollos is a model of what has been repeated again and again in the history of the Church. Numerous examples could be cited, but let us briefly recall how the Holy Spirit used the Word to further the growth of the Ancient Church in the two centuries immediately after the ministry of Apollos.

Sociologist Rodney Stark has estimated that Christianity grew in the first three centuries from roughly a few thousand believers around 40AD, comprising .0017% of the population—based on an estimated population of 60 million—to over 6,000,000 by 300AD, roughly 10.5% of the total population, assuming the size of the population remained fairly stable.[39] By the middle of the third century, Origen (*c*.185–254), an Alexandrian theologian like Apollos, could

---

[37] Bruce, *Men and Movements*, 85.

[38] See the similar theme at work in Luke's account of Stephen: Acts 6:8–10.

[39] *The Rise of Christianity. A Sociologist Reconsiders History* (Princeton: Princeton University Press, 1996), 7. For different figures, see Alan Kreider, "Worship and Evangelism in Pre-Christendom," *Vox Evangelica* 24 (1994): 7–8.

write without fear of contradiction that there was a "multitude of people coming to the faith."[40]

Why did such growth take place? While a number of reasons need to be cited to answer this question, central to this growth in the size of the church—in a day when the only public mass evangelism was when the martyrs shared their faith before death—were the Scriptures. English Bible scholar Michael Green, commenting on this fact, notes:

> From the Acts of the Apostles down to … Origen we find the same story repeated time and again. Discussion with Christians, arguments with them, annoyance at them, could lead enquirers to read these "barbaric writings" [i.e. the Scriptures] for themselves. And once they began to read, the Scriptures exercised their own fascination and power. Many an interested enquirer like Justin and Tatian, Athenagoras and Theophilus, came to Christian belief through finding, as he read, that "the Word of God is living and active and sharper than any two-edged sword" and that "the sacred Scriptures are able to instruct you for salvation through faith in Jesus Christ."[41]

One early Christian who knew the power and impact of the Word of God in his life was Hilary, born between 310 and 315 into a non-Christian home in Poitiers, Aquitaine, and who died in either 367 or 368. He probably became a Christian in his early twenties and went on to serve as a Christian bishop and author. In a very important book that he wrote entitled *On the Trinity* (356–360), he recalled at the beginning of the book how he had been led to Christ.

---

[40] *Against Celsus* 3.9.

[41] *Evangelism in the Early Church* (Rev. ed.; Grand Rapids: Wm. B. Eerdmans, 2004), 352.

He records that he had been seeking for truth amidst the various religious options in the Roman world,[42] when, in his words, he "chanced upon those books which according to Jewish tradition were written by Moses and the Prophets," namely, the Old Testament.[43] As he read them, he became convinced that there is one true God, the Maker and origin of all things, who fills the entire universe, but who cannot be identified with his creation.[44] This knowledge, he tells us, filled his soul with joy.[45] It was a knowledge he readily confessed God had taught him.[46] But he longed for more. He longed, in his words, for a "hope of everlasting happiness." For, he reasoned, what good would there be in "thinking correctly about God if death were to destroy all sensation" and all thought. In fact, he began to think that it would not be right for God to have given him knowledge about his aseity, omnipotence and omnipresence if "his life might one day end and his death last for all eternity."[47]

Hilary does not tell us how it was that he began to read the New Testament, what he calls "the evangelical and apostolic doctrine."[48] But he did, and he began to read in the Gospel of John, the first chapter, verses 1 to 14. As he read of the fact that God made the universe by One who is here called the Word and who came into this world and took on human flesh, Hilary says "my fearful and anxious soul found greater hope than it had anticipated."[49] He now realized that while there is only one God, within the Godhead there is the Father and the Son. Although no

---

[42] *On the Trinity* 1.1–4.

[43] *On the Trinity* 1.5, trans. Stephen McKenna, *Saint Hilary of Poitiers: The Trinity* (New York: Fathers of the Church, Inc., 1954), 6.

[44] *On the Trinity* 1.5–6.

[45] *On the Trinity* 1.7–8.

[46] *On the Trinity* 6.19.

[47] *On the Trinity* 1.9–10, trans. McKenna, *Saint Hilary of Poitiers: The Trinity*, 10.

[48] *On the Trinity* 1.10, trans. McKenna, *Saint Hilary of Poitiers: The Trinity*, 10.

[49] *On the Trinity* 1.10–11, trans. McKenna, *Saint Hilary of Poitiers: The Trinity*, 11.

mention is made of the Holy Spirit at this point in his account, Hilary does later indicate his deep conviction that the Spirit is a third member of the Triune Godhead.[50] Hilary also came to see that it was the Son who took on human flesh in order that human beings might become the children of God.[51] More than that, as Hilary read the New Testament he came to see that the reason the Word or the Son, or as he is often called in the New Testament, the Lord Jesus Christ, came into this world was so that he might die for sinners like himself so that:

> we may be raised from death to immortality with him. For, he received the flesh of sin that by assuming our flesh he might forgive our sin, but, while he takes our flesh, he does not share in our sin. By his death he destroyed the sentence of death ... He allows himself to be nailed to the cross in order that by the curse of the cross all the curses of our earthly condemnation might be nailed to it and obliterated. ... Hence, we are born again by God in Christ through his death.[52]

Hilary was well aware that human reason cannot ultimately comprehend such "deeds of God," and that such things must be embraced by faith. These things, he came to see, were higher than human reason but that once he believed them he then understood.[53] In Hilary's words, "the obedience of faith carries us beyond the natural power of [mere human] comprehension."[54]

So, at last, he said, "my soul was at rest," conscious now of his security in Christ and "full of joy" as he contemplated the

---

[50] *On the Trinity* 1.36.

[51] *On the Trinity* 1.11.

[52] *On the Trinity* 1.13, trans. McKenna, *Saint Hilary of Poitiers: The Trinity*, 14–15, altered.

[53] *On the Trinity* 1.13, 12.

[54] *On the Trinity* 1.37, trans. McKenna, *Saint Hilary of Poitiers: The Trinity*, 34.

future. He began to share with others what he had come to believe for himself that they too might be saved.[55] And he could now say that he had no greater reward than to serve God by proclaiming him to a world that did not know him.[56]

---

[55] *On the Trinity* 1.14.
[56] *On the Trinity* 1.37.

6

"THE SPIRIT OF SUPPLICATIONS": LEARNING ABOUT PRAYER FROM JUDE AND ZECHARIAH

And I will pour upon the house of David,
and upon the inhabitants of Jerusalem,
the spirit of grace and supplications:
and they shall look upon me whom they
have pierced, and they shall mourn for him,
as one mourneth for his only son,
and shall be in bitterness for him,
as one that is in bitterness for his firstborn.

Zechariah 12:10 KJV.

"The most neglected book in the New Testament" is the way that one writer has described the letter of Jude.[1] Such neglect is a great pity, for, as part of the canon of God's Word, Jude is "profitable for doctrine, for reproof, for correction, for instruction in righteousness."[2] Now, crucial for a proper understanding of this letter is careful attention to its structure. In verse 3, Jude issues an appeal for his readers to "contend earnestly for the faith which was once for all delivered to the saints."[3] Then, in verse 4, he proceeds to indicate why he is issuing this appeal: "Certain men have crept in unnoticed, who long ago were marked out for this

---

[1] Douglas J. Rowston, "The Most Neglected Book in the New Testament," *New Testament Studies* 21 (1974–1975): 554–563.

[2] 2 Timothy 3:16 NKJV.

[3] NKJV.

83

condemnation, ungodly men, who turn the grace of our God into lewdness and deny the only Lord God and our Lord Jesus Christ."[4]

The verses that follow this statement, verses 5 through 19, go on to provide a full-length portrait of these false teachers. It is not until verse 20, however, that Jude returns to the theme of verse 3 and explains what is entailed in contending for "the faith that was once for all delivered to the saints." Thus, verses 5 to 19 "are intended to awaken Jude's readers to the dangerous reality of their situation which makes Jude's appeal necessary."[5] It is only when Jude has outlined the serious situation which has called forth his letter that he gives positive directions on to how to face this situation. Seen in this light, verses 20–23 constitute the very climax of the letter.[6]

If this basic structure of the letter is overlooked, one easily comes away with the impression that the chief means in opposing heresy is verbal denunciation of heretics.[7] Not so. The major way to resist doctrinal and moral error is to put into practice the admonitions of verses 20–23, in particular, those of verses 20–21. While verses 22 and 23 delineate the attitude which the Christian community is to take towards false teachers and those who have come under their influence, it is in verses 20–21 that Jude prescribes the antidote to error:

> Beloved, building yourselves up on your most holy faith; praying in the Holy Spirit, keep yourselves in the love of God, looking for the mercy of our Lord Jesus Christ unto eternal life.[8]

---

[4] NKJV.

[5] Richard J. Bauckham, *Jude, 2 Peter* (Waco: Word Books, 1983), 32.

[6] Bauckham, *Jude, 2 Peter*, 111.

[7] Cf. Bauckham, *Jude, 2 Peter*, 32.

[8] NKJV.

Of the four admonitions contained in these verses it is the second one which is probably the most difficult to interpret. What exactly does Jude mean when he urges his readers to pray in the Holy Spirit (verse 20)?

Well, first, whatever its precise meaning, it definitely presents a contrast to the graphic statement with which Jude has just concluded verse 19. There Jude is able to declare with confidence that the false teachers about whom he is warning his fellow believers are men devoid of the Spirit of God. It is quite probable that these false teachers claimed to be spiritual men, men who possessed the Spirit of God.[9] Possibly they connected this claim to the fact that they were the recipients of visions, a point to which Jude alludes when he describes them as dreamers in verse 8.[10] Be this as it may, Jude does not hesitate to deny their claims. For a careful observation of their lifestyle reveals not the fruit of holiness, but immorality, the end product of ungodly desires (verses 4, 16, 18).[11] To Jude such a lifestyle was impossible for men who had drunk deeply of the Spirit of God, whose preeminent characteristic is holiness (see 1 Thessalonians 4:3–8, especially verse 8). It naturally follows that the false teachers, as men devoid of the Spirit, could not possibly fulfill Jude's exhortation to pray in the Spirit.[12]

Now, there are some authors who feel that by praying in the Spirit a special type of prayer is being indicated, namely, praying in tongues. According to this interpretation Jude is urging his readers to include praying in tongues as part of their arsenal in the

---

[9] I. Howard Marshall, *Kept by the Power of God. A Study of Perseverance and Falling Away* (Minneapolis, 1969), 163; Bauckham, *Jude, 2 Peter*, 106.

[10] J.N.D. Kelly, *A Commentary on the Epistles of Peter and Jude* (1969 ed.; repr. Grand Rapids, 1981), 260-261; Bauckham, *Jude, 2 Peter*, 106. For a different interpretation of this phrase, see Joseph B. Mayor, *The Epistle of St. Jude and the Second Epistle of St. Peter* (1907 ed.; repr. Minneapolis: Klock & Klock, 1978), 33, 74.

[11] Bauckham, *Jude, 2 Peter*, 106-107.

[12] Kelly, *Peter and Jude*, 286.

fight against heresy. But, if this were the case, Jude certainly hints at it in a rather obscure fashion.[13] Moreover, when the Apostle Paul, in Ephesians 6:18, also urges believers to pray in the Spirit, he adds a significant qualifier: *"With all prayer and petition* pray at all times in the Spirit."[14] Every conceivable type of prayer which a believer might pray, from the pastoral prayer in worship to the simple cry from the heart "Help!" is to be uttered in the Spirit.[15] Praying in the Spirit entails far more than that activity known as "praying in tongues." Nor is it, as a Canadian author has argued, "simply surrendering to the Spirit when we pray, forsaking any self-effort."[16] For prayer does require strenuous effort.[17]

Prayer in the Spirit: its meaning

What then does Jude mean when he exhorts his fellow believers to make prayer in the Spirit an integral part of their lives?

Well, first of all, the phrase "in the Spirit" is designed to draw forth the realization that there is a vast difference between prayer in the Spirit and prayer that is not in the Spirit. The difference? Prayer in the Spirit reaches the ear of God, for it goes "through Christ," whereas prayer that is not in the Spirit does neither. Jude 20 needs to be linked with Paul's statement in Ephesians 2:18: "through him (that is, Christ) we ... have our access in one Spirit to the Father," which will be discussed below. Suffice

---

[13] Michael C. Griffiths, *Three Men Filled With the Spirit. The Gift of Tongues: Must it divide us?* (London, 1969), 44; David M. Stanley, *Boasting in the Lord. The Phenomenon of Prayer in Saint Paul* (New York/Paramus/Toronto, 1973), 102–103.

[14] NASB.

[15] Markus Barth, *Ephesians: Translation and Commentary on Chapters 4-6* (Garden City: Doubleday & Co., 1974), 778; D.M. Lloyd-Jones, *The Christian Soldier. An Exposition of Ephesians 6:10 to 20* (Grand Rapids: Baker Book House, 1978), 343–344.

[16] Barry Smith, "Praying in the Spirit" *Atlantic Baptist* (December, 1990): 23.

[17] See Romans 15:30.

it to say at this point that "praying in the Spirit" means "seeking, claiming, and making use of our access to God through Christ."[18]

Second, prayer in the Spirit is inseparably yoked to a deep awareness of the fatherhood of God. When a person prays in the Spirit he or she is vividly conscious that the God to whom he or she is praying is not a distant figure, but One who is very close, in fact, One who is his or her Father. The open-membership Baptist John Bunyan (1628–1688), speaking of this aspect of prayer in the Spirit, could declare:

> Here is the life of Prayer, when in, or with the Spirit, a man being made sensible of sin, and how to come to the Lord for mercy; he comes, I say, in the strength of the Spirit, and cryeth, *Father*.
>
> That one word spoken in Faith, is better than a thousand prayers, as men call them, written and read, in a formal, cold, luke-warm way.[19]

This conviction that those who are indwelt by the Spirit of Christ can approach God as their Father with freedom and reverent familiarity was one of the key Biblical truths rediscovered at the time of the Reformation. According to H. Wace, "one thing was the centre of all the life and all the teaching of the Reformers—that God was speaking to them as their reconciled Father, and that they were in direct communion with Him."[20] The testimony of Veit Dietrich to the manner of prayer of the German Reformer Martin Luther offers an excellent illustration of this point:

---

[18] J.I. Packer, *Keep In Step With The Spirit* (Old Tappan: Fleming H. Revell Co., 1984), 79.

[19] *John Bunyan: The Doctrine of the Law and Grace unfolded and I will pray with the Spirit*, ed. Richard L. Greaves (Oxford: Clarendon Press, 1976), 252.

[20] Cited Geoffrey F. Nuttall, *The Holy Spirit in Puritan Faith and Experience* (2nd ed.; Oxford: Basil Blackwell, 1947), 63.

He prays as devoutly as one who is conversing with God, and with such hope and faith as one who addresses his father. "I know," said he, "that thou art our God and Father ..." When I heard him utter these words ... my heart burned within me for great joy, because of the familiar and devout tones in which he spoke with God.[21]

Third, prayer in the Spirit is prayer that the Spirit empowers and directs.[22] For most of us regular, private prayer is the most difficult aspect of our lives as Christians. The reason is not hard to find. As Richard Lovelace astutely notes: "our fallen nature is actually allergic to God and never wants to get too close to him. Thus, our fallen nature constantly pulls us away from prayer."[23] Specifically, prayer reveals the believer's innate poverty as well as his dependence on Another. More than anything else prayer makes us conscious of our limitations and weakness. Naturally, we tend to shy away from such a revelation. So it is that we need the Spirit's empowering in prayer, both to pray and to persevere in prayer. Here, though, one must heed the words of Andrew Fuller, the eighteenth-century Baptist theologian, who, commenting on the very phrase we are considering from Jude 20, states:

The assistance of the Holy Spirit ... is not that of which we are always sensible. We must not live in the neglect of prayer at any time because we are unconscious of being under Divine influence, but rather, as our Lord directs, pray *for* his Holy Spirit. It is *in* prayer that the Spirit of God ordinarily assists us. Prayers begun in

---

[21] Cited John G. Morris, coll. and arr., *Quaint Sayings and Doings Concerning Luther* (Philadelphia: Lindsay & Blakiston, 1859), 133.

[22] See the discussions by Lloyd-Jones, *Christian Soldier*, 349 and Bauckham, *Jude, 2 Peter*, 113.

[23] *Dynamics of Spiritual Life* (Downers Grove: InterVarsity Press, 1979), 155.

dejection have often ended in joy and praise; of this many of the Psalms of David furnish us with examples.[24]

A desire to be led by the Holy Spirit in prayer does not entail forsaking all effort in prayer and "simply surrendering to the Spirit." Rather, it should actually lead one to increasingly give oneself to prayer, and so experience the empowering of God the Holy Spirit *as* he or she prays.

What then does Jude mean when he urges his readers to pray in the Holy Spirit? Nothing less than to experience true prayer as we are brought by the Holy Spirit into the presence of God our Father to hear his voice address us through the Spirit of his Son, and to speak with him with boldness and reverence. Without such praying, Jude assures us, the defense of orthodoxy will avail for little.

Mentors in prayer: the Puritans

One group of men and women in the history of the Church who can help us enormously in this area of prayer are the Puritans. As men and women who sought to frame their lives according to God's Word,[25] they were, in the words of John Geree (*c*.1601–1649), "much in prayer."[26] Now, the Puritans had inherited a deep interest in the Holy Spirit from the Reformers, especially

---

[24] *Principles and Prospects of a Servant of Christ* in *The Complete Works of the Rev. Andrew Fuller*, ed. Joseph Belcher (3rd ed.; Philadelphia, 1845), I, 343–344.

[25] The words of the Calvinistic Baptist William Kiffen (1616-1701), writing about a fellow Puritan and Baptist, John Norcott (1621-1676) are typical of Puritanism in general: "He steered his whole course by the compass of the word, making Scripture precept or example his constant rule in matters of religion. Other men's opinions or interpretations were not the standard by which he went; but, through the assistance of the Holy Spirit, he laboured to find out what the Lord himself had said in his word" (cited Joseph Ivimey, *A History of the English Baptists* [London: B.J. Holdsworth, 1823], III, 300).

[26] John Geree, *The Character of an old English Puritan or Non-Conformist* (London, 1646) in Lawrence A. Sasek, *Images of English Puritanism. A Collection of Contemporary Sources 1589-1646* (Baton Rouge: Louisiana State University Press, 1989), 209.

John Calvin, and not surprisingly they rooted their discussion and experience of prayer in the Spirit and his work. A cluster of biblical texts—the description of the Spirit as "the Spirit of grace and supplication" (Zechariah 12:10), the admonition to both "pray in the Holy Spirit" (Jude 20; cp. Ephesians 6:18) and pray for the Spirit (Luke 11:13), the experience of calling upon God as "Abba, Father" (Romans 8:15–16; Galatians 4:6), and that unique passage on the Spirit's intercessory work (Romans 8:26–27)—were central in giving shape and substance to their reflections on this vital subject.[27] In the remainder of this chapter, we will study what the Puritans had to say about prayer by means of one of these texts that explicitly links prayer to the Spirit, Zechariah 12:10.[28]

In 1657 the Congregationalist John Owen, one-time chaplain to the Puritan army of Oliver Cromwell (1599–1658), said of this verse: "that eminent place of Zech. xii.10 is always in our thoughts."[29] This is not surprising as there were a number of things in the text which were especially appealing to Owen's Puritan mind: the idea of the outpouring of the Spirit, the denotation of the Spirit as the "Spirit of grace"—a subject of perennial interest to Calvinists—the prophetic reference to the crucified Christ, and not least, the picture of the Spirit as the inspirer of prayer. Near the end of his life, Owen was able to put into print some of the fruit of what had probably been a life-long meditation on this Old Testament verse. His major treatise on prayer, *A Discourse of*

---

[27] Roy Williams, "Lessons from the Prayer Habits of the Puritans" in D.A. Carson, ed., *Teach Us To Pray: Prayer in the Bible and the World* (Carlisle: Paternoster Press/Grand Rapids: Baker Book House for the World Evangelical Fellowship, 1990), 279.

[28] For general studies of this subject, see Gordon Stevens Wakefield, *Puritan Devotion: Its Place in the Development of Christian Piety* (London: Epworth Press, 1957), 67–82; Williams, "Lessons from the Prayer Habits of the Puritans in Carson, ed., *Teach Us To Pray*, 272–285.

[29] *Of Communion with God the Father, Son, and Holy Ghost* (1657) in *The Works of John Owen*, ed. William H. Goold (1850–1853 ed.; repr. Edinburgh: Banner of Truth Trust, 1965), II, 230.

the Work of the Holy Spirit in Prayer (1682), took as its theme verse this very text.[30]

The Spirit is called a "Spirit of supplication" in this verse, Owen reasons, since he creates within believers the desire to pray as well as enabling them to engage in prayer: "he both disposeth the hearts of men to pray and enableth them so to do."[31] Left to ourselves, Owen notes, "we are averse from any converse and intercourse with God." For "there is a secret alienation working in us from all duties and immediate communion with him."[32] In other words, if the Spirit did not stir up believers to pray, the remnants of their sinful nature would keep them from communing with God.

John Bunyan, a close friend of Owen, says much the same thing in his own inimitable style. Making reference to his own experience in a tract entitled *I Will Pray with the Spirit*, which he wrote around 1662,[33] Bunyan stresses that only the Spirit can enable the believer to persevere in prayer once he or she has begun.

> May I but speak my own Experience, and from that tell you the difficulty of Praying to God as I ought; it is enough to make your poor, blind, carnal men, to entertain strange thoughts of me, For, as for my heart, when I go to pray, I find it so loth to go to God , and when it is

---

[30] For a helpful study of Owen's understanding of prayer, see Sinclair B. Ferguson, *John Owen on the Christian Life* (Edinburgh: Banner of Truth Trust, 1987), 224–231.

[31] *A Discourse of the Work of the Holy Spirit in Prayer* in *The Works of John Owen*, ed. William H. Goold (1850–1853 ed.; repr. Edinburgh: Banner of Truth Trust, 1965), IV, 260.

[32] *Discourse of the Work of the Holy Spirit in Prayer* (*Works*, IV, 257–259).

[33] For the date, see Richard L. Greaves, "Introduction" to his ed., *John Bunyan: The Doctrine of the Law and Grace unfolded and I will pray with the Spirit* (Oxford: Clarendon Press, 1976), xl–xli. Subsequent quotations from *I will pray with the Spirit* will be taken from this text, which is the latest critical edition. For a recent modernization and abridgment of *I will pray will the Spirit*, see Louis Gifford Parkhurst, Jr. ed., *Pilgrim's Prayer Book* (Wheaton: Tyndale House, 1986).

with him, so loth to stay with him, that many times I am forced in my Prayers; *first* to beg God that he would take mine heart, and set it on himself in Christ, and when it is there, that he would keep it there (Psalm 86.11). Nay, many times I know not what to pray for, I am so blind, nor how to pray I am so ignorant; only (blessed be Grace) the *Spirit helps our infirmities* [Romans 8:26].

Oh the starting-holes that the heart hath in time of Prayer! None knows how many by-wayes the heart hath, and back-lains, to slip away from the presence of God. How much pride also, if enabled with expressions? How much hypocrisie, if before others? And how little con-science is there made of Prayer between God and the Soul in secret, unless the *Spirit of Supplication* [Zechariah 12:10] be there to help?[34]

This passage displays a couple of the most attractive features of the Puritans: their transparent honesty and in-depth knowledge of the human heart. From personal experience Bunyan well knew the allergic reaction of the old nature to the presence of God. So, were it not for the Spirit, none would be able to persevere in prayer. Little wonder that Bunyan says right after the above passage, which, it should be noted, concludes with an allusion to Zechariah 12:10: "When the Spirit gets into the heart then there is prayer indeed, and not till then."[35]

The Presbyterian divine John Flavel (*c.*1630–1691), also com-menting on this verse from Zechariah, makes the same point: "The habit [of prayer] is given by the Spirit, when the principles of grace are first infused into the soul, Zech. xii.10. Acts ix.11."[36] Flavel illustrates the principle derived from Zechariah 12 with the

---

[34] *I will pray with the Spirit*, 256–257.

[35] *I will pray with the Spirit*, 257.

[36] *Preparations for Suffering, or The Best Work in the Worst Times* in *The Works of John Flavel* (1820 ed.; repr. London: The Banner of Truth Trust, 1968), VI, 66.

statement that is made by the Lord to Ananias about the Apostle Paul immediately after he experienced the grace of God on the Damascus Road. "Behold," Ananias is told, "he is praying." We see the same combination of texts in Flavel's fellow Presbyterian Thomas Manton (1620–1677):

> Habitual grace is necessary to prayer: Zech. xii.10, "I will pour upon them a spirit of grace and supplication." Where there is *grace* there will be *supplication*. As soon as we are new born we fall a-crying; "Behold, he prayeth," Acts ix.11, is the first news we hear of Paul after his conversion.[37]

Finally, to Christians who say that they cannot pray, Thomas Brooks (1608–1680), a popular Puritan preacher in London during the 1640s and 1650s, responds with the verse we have been looking at from Zechariah. Surely this text indicates, he argues in *The Privie Key of Heaven; or, Twenty Arguments for Closet-Prayer* (1665), that all genuine believers are indwelt by the Spirit. And because the Spirit who indwells them is "a Spirit of prayer and supplication," they must then be able to pray.[38] In fact, Brooks is convinced on the basis of this text that "the more any man is now under the blessed pouring out of the Spirit of Christ, the more that man gives himself up to secret communion with Christ."[39]

---

[37] *An Exposition of the Epistle of Jude* (London: The Banner of Truth Trust, 1958), 338.

[38] *The Privie Key of Heaven; or, Twenty Arguments for Closet-Prayer* in *The Works of Thomas Brooks*, ed. Alexander B. Grosart (1861–1867 ed., rerpr. Edinburgh: Banner of Truth Trust, 1980), II, 225.

[39] *Privie Key of Heaven* in *Works*, II, 297.

7
EXPECTING THE SPIRIT[1]

*Praying for souls is a main stroke in the winning of souls. ...
Yea, who can tell, how far the prayers of the saints, & of a few saints,
may prevail with heaven to obtain that grace, that shall win whole
peoples and kingdoms to serve the Lord? ... It may be, the nations of
the world, would quickly be won from the idolatries of paganism, and
the impostures of Mahomet, if a Spirit of prayer, were at work among
the people of God.*

Cotton Mather
(1663–1728)

One of the drawbacks of modern English diction is that it is unable to distinguish between the plural and singular forms of a verb or pronoun in the second person. Unlike other European languages, for instance French with its various forms of *tu* and *vous*, modern English has to make do with the forms of one word for both the singular and plural: "you." This lack causes some definite problems in the translation of the Greek of the New Testament, since the latter does make clear distinctions between the plural and singular forms of the verb, possessive adjective, and pronoun in the second person. In most cases this weakness of the English language makes no appreciable difference in the understanding of the

---

[1] Most of the material in this chapter originally appeared as "Praying for Revival: is it Biblical?" *Reformation Today* 115 (May–June 1990): 10–14. Used by permission. The title for this chapter was suggested by a conversation with Pastor Tim Kerr of Richmond Hill, Ontario.

New Testament text. But, in some cases, this weakness actually obscures the import of the text. This can be readily seen in the interpretation of Philemon 22, "prepare a guest room for me, for I trust that through your prayers I shall be granted to you."

Paul's letter to Philemon is in the main a private one, in which the Apostle Paul takes up the subject of Philemon's runaway slave Onesimus with discretion and tact. After the mention of other Christians in the salutation and initial benediction (verses 1–3), Paul addresses himself in the body of the letter to one individual, namely Philemon. Thus, underlying all of the words translated by the English you or your from verse 4 to 22a is either a Greek verb in the second person singular or a form of the possessive adjective or personal pronoun in the second person singular. But, then, in the middle of verse 22 there is a sudden shift from the second person singular to the second person plural. Paul asks Philemon to prepare a guest-room for him. The Apostle then goes on to give the reason for this request: "I trust that through your prayers I shall be granted to you." Without warning Paul switches over to using forms of the second person plural personal pronoun. This shift, hidden in nearly all modern English translations of the verse, is not a fortuitous one nor one that is done merely for stylistic effect. Behind it lies a profound appreciation of corporate prayer.

Although the body of the letter is directed to Philemon, since Paul is dealing with a personal matter which primarily concerns him, Paul never forgets that Philemon also belongs to a circle of believers who meet in his home as a house-church. Now, at the conclusion of the letter, Paul informs Philemon of his intention to visit him and his assurance that the believers who comprise the house-church which meets in Philemon's home are regularly remembering him in prayer (verse 22). The communal context of this letter, reflected in verses 1 and 2, now suddenly re-emerges. As Paul thinks of Philemon praying for his release from prison and his forthcoming visit to his home, he cannot isolate Philemon's prayers from those of his fellow believers. Paul's reliance on other believers in his ministry is again evident as he mentions his assurance that not only Philemon, but also his entire house-church is remembering him in prayer. Furthermore, the context for these prayers should not be regarded as limited to these believers' personal times of prayer. Paul's language envisages the house-church in Philemon's home praying as a whole and together for his release. As the eighteenth-century Baptist commentator John Gill (1697-1771) puts it: "the prayer of a righteous man availeth much with God, and is very prevalent with him, and much more the prayers of a whole church."

Corinth

Another classic example of Paul's convictions regarding corporate prayer is found in relation to one of the major cities in the ancient world, Corinth. This Greek city was one of the worst for immorality and flagrant sin. Poised at the centre of trade routes that ran from the western to the eastern Mediterranean, the city prospered greatly. But along with wealth and luxury came vice and decadence. In fact, the Greeks had coined a verb, "to Corinthianize," that is, "to live like a Corinthian," which meant to be sexually immoral.[2] This verb alone speaks volumes about the state of the city. One gets another picture of the normal activities of city life in Corinth in Paul's first letter to the Corinthians.

---

[2] Richard N. Longenecker, "Acts" in Frank E. Gaebelein, *et al.*, eds., *The Expositor's Bible Commentary* (Grand Rapids: Zondervan Publishing House, 1981), 9:480.

> Do you not know that the unrighteous will not inherit the kingdom of God? Do not be deceived. Neither fornicators, nor idolaters, nor adulterers, nor homosexuals, nor sodomites, nor thieves, nor covetous, nor drunkards, nor revilers, nor extortioners will inherit the kingdom of God. And such were some of you.[3]

As Paul implies in verse 11, all of the sinful practices listed in the previous two verses were commonplace in Corinth; they were all part of a day's activities. Yet, if we read the account of Paul's ministry in Corinth in Acts 18, one sees that this sinkhole of sin and immorality presented no problem for the living God, who created the heavens and the earth and all that is in them. For Acts 18 describes a revival in this city of decadence. Two aspects of this revival bear further study.

First, what were the roots of the revival? What preparation had there been for this deep work of God? One item is especially prominent: prayer. In his biography of Asahel Nettleton (1783–1844), the American evangelist who knew genuine revival in his ministry, Bennet Tyler noted: "When God pours out his Spirit he usually first revives his work in the hearts of his own people, and … awakens and converts sinners in answer to their prayers."[4]

Then, what were the effects of the revival? How did God answer the prayers of his people?

Praying for Spirit-wrought revival

Robert Jewett dates Paul's arrival at Corinth in the winter of 49–50.[5] A few months later, probably in March or April of 50, he was joined by his two fellow-workers, Silas and Timothy (see Acts

---

[3] 1 Corinthians 6:9–11a NKJV.

[4] *Nettleton and His Labours. The Memoir of Dr. Ashael Nettleton*, ed. Andrew A. Bonar (1854 ed.; repr. Edinburgh/Carlisle: The Banner of Truth Trust, 1975), 296.

[5] *The Thessalonian Correspondence* (Philadelphia: Fortress Press, 1986), 60.

18:5). Timothy came from a church which Paul had planted a year or so earlier in Thessalonica in northern Greece (see 1 Thessalonians 3:2, 8). It appears that he arrived with questions from the Thessalonian believers and a report of problems in their church. Paul's response was to write the letter we now know as 1 Thessalonians.

Roughly five to seven weeks later he wrote a second letter to this church: 2 Thessalonians. This second letter was mostly devoted to the subject of the last days, but in chapter 3 Paul makes a very interesting and highly significant request of the Thessalonian believers: he asks them to pray for his ministry at Corinth: "Finally, brethren, pray for us, that the word of the Lord may run swiftly and be glorified, just as it is with you, and that we may be delivered from unreasonable and wicked men; for not all have faith."[6] Here, Paul requests prayer regarding two items: the progress of the gospel and the opposition to the gospel.

What is Paul specifically requesting in these two items? The first request relates to the triumphant progress of the gospel. The Thessalonians are asked to pray that "the word of the Lord may run *swiftly* and be glorified just as *it is* with you."[7] What an odd image: the word of the Lord running swiftly! Immersed as he was in the Old Testament, Paul almost certainly has in mind a text from the Psalms, namely, Psalm 147:15, where we read: "He sends out His command to the earth; His word runs very swiftly."[8] In this verse "the psalmist glories in Yahweh's word of power. He issues his command and it is executed; he speaks and ... it is done."[9]

---

[6] 2 Thessalonians 3:1–2 NKJV.

[7] NKJV.

[8] NKJV.

[9] Leslie C. Allen, *Psalms 101–150* (Waco: Word Books, 1983), 310.

The verses that immediately follow in Psalm 147 reinforce verse 15: "He gives snow like wool; he scatters the frost like ashes; he casts out his hail like morsels; who can stand before his cold?"[10] Severe winter conditions as are described in these verses were, and are, rare in Palestine. But the Psalmist delights in them like a North American child romping in the snow, for he sees the irresistible power of the God of Jacob in the snowflakes, the frost and the icy hailstones. He sees in the weather of winter far more than the elements of nature; he discerns the hand of a Sovereign God: "He sends out His command to the earth; His word runs very swiftly. ... Who can stand before his cold?"[11] In like fashion Paul urges the Thessalonians to pray that God would cause his Word, the gospel, to work with irresistible power in the lives and hearts of sinful men and women in Corinth. Pray, Paul is saying, that the warmth of the gospel would melt the ice-cold hearts of pagans in Corinth and cause them to be alive to God.

He also asks his Thessalonian friends to pray that the "word of the Lord ... might be glorified." What does the Apostle mean by this phrase? "Be glorified" is normally an expression used with reference to God or Christ.[12] Here, though, it appears to refer to the way the gospel is received and treated. Pray, Paul asks, that the Word of God might be received with reverence and obeyed. The phrase "just as it is with you" would remind the Thessalonians of the way that they had received the Word of God: "For this reason we also thank God without ceasing, because when you received the Word of God which you heard from us, you welcomed it not as the word of men, but as it is in truth, the word of God,

---

[10] Psalm 147:16–17 NKJV.

[11] NKJV.

[12] William Neil, *The Epistle of Paul to the Thessalonians* (London: Hodder and Stoughton, 1950), 187.

which also effectively works in you who believe."[13] Pray, Paul urges the believers in Thessalonica, that the Corinthians might receive God's Word in just the same way as you did. Paul's request here reflects the conviction that, as John Calvin would later state:

> As God alone is a fit witness of himself in his Word, so also the word will not find acceptance in men's hearts before it is sealed by the inward testimony of the Spirit. … [Scripture] seriously affects us only when it is sealed upon our hearts through the Spirit.[14]

In one word, for what is Paul asking? Revival![15] He is asking the Thessalonians to pray that God would sovereignly move in the hearts of unbelievers in Corinth and give them a hunger for the Word of God, give them a love for it, cause them to reverence it, and eagerly embrace its truth about themselves and about Christ. The very way that Paul asks the Thessalonians to pray for this work of God shows his clear awareness that revival does not come through human engineering. Rather, the Apostle clearly believes it is a sovereign work of God in response to the prayers of his people. Revival, renewal, is God's work, and unless God draws men and women to himself, none will be converted.

Does that mean then that we sit back, put our feet up, and do nothing? By no means, Paul says. Pray! Pray that God the Holy Spirit would clear away the fog that binds people to the truth of the gospel, that he would show sinners their sin and rebellion before God and melt their icy-hearts that they would be moved to

---

[13] 1 Thessalonians 2:13 NKJV.

[14] *Institutes* 1.7.4, 5, trans. Ford Lewis Battles in his and John T. McNeill, *Calvin: Institutes of the Christian Religion* (Philadelphia: The Westminster Press, 1960), 1:79, 80.

[15] Compare the remarks of J.I. Packer, *God In Our Midst* (Ann Arbor: Servant Books, 1987), 34.

cry out to Christ for salvation. Expect the Spirit to move, Paul is urging his readers then—and now!

Paul's second request is closely bound up with the first, for wherever the Spirit makes the truths of the gospel relevant and alive, there will be opposition. Pray, Paul asks his brothers and sisters in northern Greece, that he and his companions, Silas and Timothy, "may be delivered from unreasonable and wicked men; for not all have faith."[16] Paul has in mind some specific adversaries of the gospel. Turning to Acts 18, we find them identified in verses 5–6:

> When Silas and Timothy had come from Macedonia, Paul was constrained by the Spirit, and testified to the Jews that Jesus is the Christ. But when they opposed him and blasphemed, he shook his garments and said to them, "Your blood be upon your own heads; I am clean. From now on I will go to the Gentiles."[17]

Pray, Paul asks, that this opposition will not hinder the spread of the faith. It needs noting that the Thessalonian Church knew of such opposition from personal experience, opposition that led to persecution and affliction for the believers.[18]

Revival and its fruit

Did God answer these prayers of the Thessalonian believers on behalf of Paul's mission in the city of Corinth and if so, how? For the answer to the second request one can look at Acts 18:12–16:

---

16 2 Thessalonians 3:2 NKJV.
17 NKJV.
18 2 Thessalonians 1:3–4.

> And when Gallio was proconsul of Achaia, the Jews with one accord rose up against Paul and brought him to the judgment seat, saying, "This fellow persuades men to worship God contrary to the law." And when Paul was about to open his mouth, Gallio said to the Jews, "If it were a matter of wrongdoing or wicked crimes, O Jews, there would be reason why I should bear with you. But if it is question of words and names and your own law, look to it yourselves; for I do not want to be a judge of such matters." And he drove them from the judgment seat.[19]

Paul's request that he and his companions be "freed from unreasonable and wicked men" found a clear answer in Gallio's refusal to listen to the Jewish charge against Paul. Lucius Junius Annaeus Gallio (d.65) was the most powerful Roman politician Paul had met to this point in his life.[20] He was the younger brother of Seneca (d.65), who was the tutor of the emperor Nero (37–68). As such, Gallio's decisions carried great weight and legal precedence. By refusing to involve the Roman state in what he considered to be an internal Jewish quarrel, Gallio set an important precedent which would allow the Church to expand without interference from the Roman state, at least for another fifteen years or so.

In other words, as believers prayed in Thessalonica, God moved in the halls of power and caused a pagan Roman governor, Gallio, to show favor to his man in Corinth, Paul, and so allowed the gospel free course in the city. No wonder that Paul, a number of years later, urged prayer for those in authority as a priority of the church (see Timothy 2:1–2), for, by the Spirit's power, prayer changes history.

---

[19] NKJV.

[20] On Gallio's career, see Longenecker, "Acts," 485. See also J.H. Harrop, "Gallio" in J.D. Douglas, *et al.*, eds., *The Illustrated Bible Dictionary* (Leicester: InterVarsity Press/Wheaton: Tyndale House/Lane Cove: Hodder & Stoughton, 1980), 1:538.

But what of the other prayer request—that revival would come to Corinth? Again, look at Acts 18:

> When Silas and Timothy had come from Macedonia, Paul was constrained by the Spirit, and testified to the Jews that Jesus is the Christ. But when they opposed him and blasphemed, he shook his garments and said to them, "Your blood be upon your own heads; I am clean. From now on I will go to the Gentiles." And he departed from there and entered the house of a certain man named Justus, one who worshipped God, whose house was next door to the synagogue. Then Crispus, the ruler of the synagogue, believed on the Lord with all his household. And many of the Corinthians, hearing, believed and were baptized.[21]

A multitude of Corinthians were converted, including Crispus, the leader or ruler of the synagogue.

Further evidence of the way that God moved at Corinth is found in the text that was cited at the beginning of this chapter:

> Do you not know that the unrighteous will not inherit the kingdom of God? Do not be deceived. Neither fornicators, nor idolaters, nor adulterers, nor homosexuals, nor sodomites, nor thieves, nor covetous, nor drunkards, nor revilers, nor extortioners will inherit the kingdom of God. And such were some of you. But you were washed, but you were sanctified, but you were justified in the name of the Lord Jesus and by the Spirit of our God.[22]

Here is a graphic description of the depth of the Holy Spirit's work. J.B. Phillips, who is best known for his paraphrase of the

---

[21] Acts 18:5–8 NKJV.
[22] 1 Corinthians 6:9–11 NKJV.

New Testament, says of verse 11 in his autobiography, *The Price of Success*: "I think that this single sentence is one of the most important ever written."[23] One can see why Phillips came to this conclusion when verses 9–10 are studied in their historical context and it is seen what God did in the lives of the Corinthian believers.

The sexually immoral, those involved in the worship of false gods, those who were adulterers, male homosexuals and their effeminate lovers, thieves, those whose religion was the acquisition of money and possessions, alcoholics, those whose mouths regularly spewed forth abuse and slander, swindlers—none were able to stand before the irresistible Breath of God: "And such were some of you. But you were washed, but you were sanctified, but you were justified in the name of the Lord Jesus and by the Spirit of our God."[24] These sinners were cleansed from their guilt and shame, and their sins, like filth, had been washed away. Those who had devoted themselves to sin and shameful deeds were now set apart to be used for God's glory. They were clothed in the seamless robe of Christ's righteousness.

Expecting the Spirit

God does not promise that wherever there is prayer for revival there will be revival.[25] But 2 Thessalonians 3:1–2 and Acts 18 do demonstrate what is generally the relationship between prayer and revival: without prayer, there will be no revival. This is a truism which finds ample confirmation in a number of other Scriptural texts. For instance, in Ezekiel 36:37, God's people are encouraged to pray for the restoration of their nation, even though the

---

[23] *The Price of Success* (London: Hodder and Stoughton, 1984), 147.

[24] 1 Corinthians 6:11 NKJV.

[25] This fact is brought out forcibly by Iain H. Murray, "The Necessary Ingredients of a Biblical Revival," *The Banner of Truth* 184 (January 1979): 21. This article is very helpful with regard to the whole matter of revival.

previous verses, verses 33–36, indicate that this restoration was something God had already sovereignly ordained. Or consider the outpouring of the Spirit at Pentecost, which, though secured by the sufferings of Christ, was a donation given to believers who "continued with one accord in prayer and supplication"[26]

Church history also bears witness to the importance of prayer in relationship to revival. For example, in 1784, a group of English Calvinistic Baptists, acting upon the proposal of John Sutcliff, pastor of the Baptist Church in Olney, Buckinghamshire, established a regular prayer meeting for revival on the first Monday evening of every month.[27] Eight years later William Carey, a former member of the Baptist Church in Olney and subsequently a missionary to India, could state of these prayer meetings:

> I trust our monthly prayer-meetings for the success of the gospel have not been in vain. It is true a want of importunity too generally attends our prayers; yet unimportunate, and feeble as they have been, it is to be believed that God has heard, and in a measure answered them. The churches that have engaged in the practice have in general since that time been evidently on the increase; ... there are calls to preach the gospel in many places where it has not been usually published; yea, a glorious door is opened, and is likely to be opened wider and wider ... These are events that ought not to be overlooked; they are not to be reckoned small things; and yet perhaps they are small compared with what might have been expected, if all had cordially entered into the spirit

---

[26] Acts 1:14 KJV. For other biblical examples, see Daniel 9; Ezra 1; and Acts 4:23–31. See also Iain H. Murray, "Prayer and Revival," *The Banner of Truth* 132 (September 1974): 20.

[27] For a fuller account, see Michael A.G. Haykin, *One heart and one soul: John Sutcliff of Olney, his friends, and his times* (Darlington: Evangelical Press, 1994), 153–171.

of the proposal, so as to have made the cause of Christ their own.[28]

Over the next few decades these churches continued to pray and a rich measure of revival came to many of them. They learned from firsthand experience the intimate relationship which the Apostle Paul draws between revival and prayer in 2 Thessalonians 3:1–2. As Thomas Blundel (*c.*1752–1824), a friend of both Sutcliff and Carey, stated in a sermon on this very text:

It is chiefly in answer to prayer that God has carried on his cause in the world: he could work without any such means; but he does not, neither will he. … He loves that his people should feel interested in his cause, and labour to promote it, though he himself worketh all in all.[29]

---

[28] *An Enquiry into the Obligations of Christians to Use Means for the Conversion of the Heathens* (Leicester: Ann Ireland, 1792), 79, 80.

[29] *The River of Life Impeded* in his *Sermons on Various Subjects* (London: J. Burditt, 1806), 183, 184.

8

Collecting money and maintaining the unity of the Spirit[1]

Be zealous to maintain the unity of the Spirit
in the bond of peace.

Ephesians 4:3.[2]

Among the most precious texts of God's Word is Ephesians 5:25b: "Christ ... loved the church and gave himself for her."[3] Before time began or space was formed, the One we know as the Lord Jesus Christ had set his heart on dying for human sinners. Not out of necessity nor from need, not by constraint nor grudgingly, but from a heart of love, out of mercy and kindness, freely and willingly, Christ came into this world to die for the church.

Equally the Holy Spirit, whom Christ gave in his stead when he ascended to the right hand of the Father, also loves the Church for which Christ died. After all it was the Spirit who laid the church's apostolic foundation on the day of Pentecost.[4] And it is the Spirit who adds men and women to the church as he enables them to confess Christ as Lord.[5] It is the Spirit who pours the love of God into their hearts and draws them to worship God and pray

---

[1] This chapter was originally given as an address at The Evangelical Movement of Wales Ministers' Conference, Bala, Wales, June 17, 2008. It has appeared as "Paul: Collecting Money and Maintaining the Unity of the Spirit," *The Banner of Truth* 541 (October 2008): 15–23. Used by permission.

[2] Author's translation.

[3] NASB.

[4] Acts 2. See also Ephesians 2:19–22; 3:5.

[5] 1 Corinthians 12:3.

109

to him as "Dear Father."[6] It is the Spirit who lavishes gifts upon the church that she might grow in spiritual maturity and bring glory to the One who is ever at the centre of all the Spirit's work, namely, the Lord Jesus.[7]

It properly follows that one of the marks of being filled with the Spirit is participation in this love of the Spirit for the Church.[8] Those who are led by the Spirit, those who are filled with the Spirit, love the people of God.

"The love of the Spirit"

The Spirit's creation of love for the people of God seems to appear in a verse in Romans 15. Paul is about to embark on a dangerous trip to Judaea and Jerusalem, where he knows he will face "unbelievers" who are strong opponents of the gospel.[9] So Paul requests his readers in Rome not to forget to pray for him. Adding to the solemnity of this appeal for prayer is the two-fold basis upon which the Apostle makes his request. First, the admonition that Paul gives to his readers is "through our Lord Jesus Christ." Here Paul invokes the authority of the one Lord, to whom both he and his readers are bound as servants.[10] He says in effect that because Christ is their Lord, they ought to pray for his servant who is seeking the advance of his Master's kingdom and the exaltation of his dear name. Then, he makes this request "by the love of the Spirit." This is a unique phrase in the Scriptures. Elsewhere when the Scriptures speak of the love of one of the divine persons, it is

---

[6] Romans 5:5; Philippians 3:3; Galatians 4:6.

[7] 1 Corinthians 12; Ephesians 4:11–13; John 16:14.

[8] 1 John 3:16–24.

[9] Romans 15:30–31.

[10] C.E.B. Cranfield, *A Critical and Exegetical Commentary on the Epistle to the Romans* (1979 ed.; repr. Edinburgh: T. & T. Clark, 1986), II, 776.

always the love of the Father or the love of Christ.[11] Moreover, it is not immediately clear what Paul means by the phrase.

- Is it the love that believers have for the Holy Spirit?
- Or the love that the Spirit has for believers?
- Or should it be understood to mean the love that the Holy Spirit produces in believers for one another?

Few commentators think that the first option is a possibility here. The second has been held by, among others, John Ryland, Jr.,[12] and John Murray (1898–1975), the Presbyterian theologian who taught at Westminster Theological Seminary for much of his life and who wrote a superb commentary on Romans.[13] The interpretation of John Calvin, though, is the one that probably makes the best sense here. He interprets the phrase as the love "by which the saints ought to embrace one another."[14] As Calvin goes on to say: "The love of the Spirit means the love by which Christ joins us together, because it is not of the flesh, nor of the world, but proceeds from His Spirit who is the bond of our unity."[15]

In this reading of the phrase, Paul is basing his appeal on the fact that his readers are indwelt by the Spirit and as such know something of the love that the Spirit produces in believers for one another. Paul thus expects that love for God's people will in part

---

[11] Gordon D. Fee, *God's Empowering Presence: The Holy Spirit in the Letters of Paul* (Peabody: Hendrickson Publishers, 1994), 632. For an exposition of the love of the Spirit for the believer that draws on a variety of biblical texts about the Spirit's work, see Robert Philip, *The Love of the Spirit Traced in His Work* (1836 ed.; repr. Grand Rapids: Reformation Heritage Books, 2006).

[12] "The Love of the Spirit" in his *Pastoral Memorials: Selected from the Manuscripts of the Late Revd. John Ryland, D.D. of Bristol* (London: B.J. Holdsworth, 1828), II, 42–43.

[13] *The Epistle to the Romans* (Grand Rapids: Wm. B. Eerdmans, 1965), 221.

[14] *The Epistles of Paul the Apostle to the Romans and to the Thessalonians*, trans. Ross Mackenzie (1960 ed.; repr. Grand Rapids: Wm. B. Eerdmans, 1973), 317. See also Fee, *God's Empowering Presence*, 633.

[15] *Epistles of Paul the Apostle to the Romans and to the Thessalonians*, 317.

be demonstrated by prayer for them. To paraphrase the Apostle John: the one who says he loves God's people and never prays for them is a liar.[16]

"Constrained by the Spirit"

Now, this trip to Jerusalem is also treated at some length by Luke in the final section of the Book of Acts. On the way to Jerusalem, Paul with his apostolic band and a few other brothers,[17] stop at Miletus, from where Paul asks the elders in Ephesus to come and meet him. As Paul meets with the Ephesian elders in Miletus, he tells them that he is "constrained by the Spirit" to go up to Jerusalem. He is not certain what awaits him there, although the Spirit has been bearing witness through various Christian prophets that he will face "imprisonment and afflictions."[18] A little further on in the journey Paul and his apostolic band reach the ancient Phoenician city of Tyre where, during a meeting with some brothers, they urge the Apostle—"through the Spirit," Luke tells us—not to go to Jerusalem.[19]

At Caesarea, yet another stop on the journey, Paul and his co-workers lodge with Philip the evangelist. While there, Paul is again warned, this time by the prophet Agabus, of what awaits him at Jerusalem. "Thus says the Holy Spirit," Agabus solemnly announces as he takes Paul's belt and binds his own hands and feet, "This is how the Jews will bind the man who owns this belt and deliver him into the hands of the Gentiles." This is too much for Paul's companions who now plead with him not to continue in the journey. But Paul, knowing that the Spirit is leading him up to Jerusalem, is determined to go on. He is ready, he tells his friends

---

[16] See also below, Chapter 11.
[17] For a list of some of those accompanying Paul, see Acts 20:4.
[18] Acts 20:22-23.
[19] Acts 21:4.

and the brothers in Caesarea, "not only to be imprisoned but even to die in Jerusalem for the name of the Lord Jesus."[20]

So, the Spirit led Paul up to Jerusalem, where he did indeed experience afflictions and imprisonment at the hands of the Romans. But—and this is vital to answer—why did the Spirit lead him up to Jerusalem? In short, the answer to this question can put this way: was it not because of the Spirit's love for the Church and especially his delight in the unity of believers in Christ?

The collection and the Spirit

Go back to Romans 15, where one discovers the reason that Paul took this dangerous trip to Jerusalem in the first place. There Paul informs the Roman believers that he is coming to Rome and that he intends to go from there to Spain. But before he headed off to Rome he first had to go up to Jerusalem.[21] As he writes in verses 25–28:

> At present, however, I am going to Jerusalem bringing aid to the saints. For Macedonia and Achaia have been pleased to make some contribution for the poor among the saints at Jerusalem. They were pleased to do it, and indeed they owe it to them. For if the Gentiles have come to share in their spiritual blessings, they ought also to be of service to them in material blessings. When therefore, I have completed this and have delivered to them what has been collected, I will leave for Spain by way of you.[22]

Paul was going up to Jerusalem to deliver a collection of money for the poor believers there. But who were these poor saints and how did they come to be poor? What were the historical circumstances

---

[20] Acts 21:13.
[21] Acts 15:23–24.
[22] ESV.

that prompted Paul to begin making such a collection as this in the first place?

To answer these questions we have to go back to the earliest days of the Jerusalem church when, soon after Pentecost, the first Christian community exuberantly sold their real estate and their personal possessions, "had all things in common," and sought to ensure that there were no poor among them.[23] In doing this, these believers were not seeking to obey any explicit commandment from Christ. Rather, they were simply motivated by a desire to make manifest and plain for all to see that in Christ they had "one heart and one soul."[24]

In disposing of their financial reserves in this way, however, the community placed itself in a highly vulnerable position. Persecution would only have aggravated this situation.[25] Moreover, during the 40s there were a series of food shortages in Palestine and then a particularly severe famine in 48AD which appears to have triggered a financial crisis in the Jerusalem church.[26] Thus, when the Apostle Paul went up to Jerusalem in the very year that this famine struck he was specifically asked by the leaders there to "remember the poor."[27]

In making this suggestion the leaders of the Jerusalem church little knew how it would become a major part of Paul's life and ministry for nearly a decade. Scott McKnight goes so far as to

---

[23] Acts 2:44–45; 4:32–35.

[24] Acts 4:32; Max Scheler, *Ressentiment*, ed. L.A. Coser and trans. W.W. Holdheim (New York: Schocken Books, 1972), 111–112.

[25] Compare the persecution described in Hebrews 10:33–34, where the loss of material possessions and goods was involved.

[26] Keith F. Nickle, *The Collection: A Study in Paul's Strategy* (Geneva: Allenson, 1966), 24, 29–32; S. McKnight, "Collection for the Saints" in *Dictionary of Paul and His Letters*, eds. Gerald F. Hawthorne and Ralph P. Martin, with Daniel G. Reid (Downers Grove/Leicester: InterVarsity Press, 1993), 144.

[27] Galatians 2:10.

describe it as "Paul's *obsession* for nearly two decades."[28] While this is probably something of an exaggeration, it clearly was of great importance to the Apostle.

This collection involved the making of elaborate plans to gather together what was a substantial amount of money from the various churches that Paul had planted among the Gentiles.[29] Then, once the money had been gathered, it was to be delivered to the Jewish believers in Jerusalem to help provide aid for the poorest of them there. But Paul came to see that this collection was a fabulous opportunity to demonstrate to the Jerusalem church and Jewish believers everywhere that even as there was one Lord and one gospel, so also there was one people of God.[30]

In Romans 15:27 the Apostle indicates succinctly what his view of the collection was: it is nothing less than a concrete and visible expression of the unity that Jewish and Gentile believers had in Christ. It was from the Jewish believers in Palestine that Paul and other missionaries to the Gentiles had been sent out to bring the light of the gospel to those who were imprisoned in the dark dungeon of paganism. In so doing the Gentiles had been partakers in their spiritual blessings. Through the witness of Jewish believers these Gentiles had been taught the things of the Spirit. Having such unity in spiritual things, it was only proper that the Gentiles minister to their Jewish brothers and sisters in material things. In fact, the word that Paul uses in Romans 15:26 to describe the collection is *koinonia*, which in other contexts in Paul's writings is translated "fellowship." The sharing by Gentile believers of their financial resources with their brothers and sisters in Palestine is not simply a gift of money and nothing more. For Paul it

---

[28] McKnight, "Collection for the Saints," 143.

[29] See 1 Corinthians 16:1–4; 2 Corinthians 8–9. The reference in 2 Corinthians 8:20 to this collection being a "lavish gift" points to the substantial amount of money involved.

[30] McKnight, "Collection for the Saints," 145.

speaks of their common life in Christ and, as such, it is a sign of fellowship, proof of their love for the brethren.[31]

It is noteworthy that in this text, his last word on the collection, Paul gives no indication that he thought this substantial gift of money would solve once and for all the financial hardship and problems of the Jerusalem believers. But he hoped and prayed that it would convince the believers in Jerusalem that just as there is one gospel and one Lord, so there is one people of God, bound together by one Spirit and demonstrating that unity in real, tangible ways. The collection had become for Paul far more than a gift to relieve poverty and physical suffering. It was nothing less than a powerful symbol of the unity of God's people in the Spirit, a unity that had been brought into being by a Spirit-empowered embrace of the gospel. The one gospel preached to different ethnic groups had produced one people of God.

As has been pointed out, in taking this collection up to Jerusalem Paul was well aware of the dangers that he faced. Thus, he asked the Roman Christians to pray fervently that his "service for Jerusalem" would be "acceptable to the saints."[32] Paul's sense of the dangers that awaited him in Jerusalem was not unfounded. After he had delivered the collection to the believers there,[33] the presence of one of his Gentile brothers with him got him into trouble. Seen by Jewish zealots in the Temple who hated him and the gospel which he preached, he was wrongly accused of defiling the Temple by bringing one of the Gentiles, the Ephesian Trophimus, into those areas of the Temple reserved for the Jews.[34] A mob

---

[31] James D. G. Dunn, *Romans 9–16* (Word Biblical Commentary, vol. 38B; Dallas: Word Publishing, 1988), 875.

[32] Romans 15:31.

[33] See Acts 24:17 for the sole reference to the actual collection in Acts.

[34] Acts 21:27–9. Trophimus had come up with Paul to Jerusalem as a representative of the churches in Asia. For the other representatives, see Acts 20:4.

sought to kill the Apostle and he was rescued only at the last moment by the Romans. Placed under arrest, he would spend the next four years as a Roman prisoner and it was in chains that he finally arrived in Rome.

"The unity of the Spirit"

One of the Apostle Paul's deepest convictions was that the death of the Lord Jesus had not only accomplished the reconciliation of God and those for whom Christ died, but it had also broken down the barriers that divide men and women from one another. This conviction first comes to expression in Galatians, where Paul asserts that in Christ Jesus "there is neither Jew nor Greek, there is neither slave nor free, there is neither male nor female."[35] In the presence of God, all men and women are on an equal footing: all are sinners and all need to come to God the same way, through faith alone in the Lord Jesus Christ alone. In the context of this letter this verse is a sharp rebuke to those individuals who were troubling the Galatian believers by urging them to believe that for salvation one had to embrace all of the distinctive features of Judaism. Not so, Paul strongly responds. Religious background, race, even gender, are meaningless issues when one stands in God's holy presence. There, one thing, and one thing alone matters: does Christ Jesus know you as his own? One's religious heritage, one's economic standing, one's gender—all fade away in the light of one's answer to that most important of all questions, "Do you know God through his Son, the Lord Jesus Christ?"

A few years later, when some Corinthian believers, "restless experientialists,"[36] had become overly impressed with one of the

---

[35] Galatians 3:28.

[36] This apt description is that of J. I. Packer, *A Quest for Godliness. The Puritan Vision of the Christian Life* (Wheaton: Crossway Books, 1990), 30.

more spectacular spiritual gifts, namely, speaking in tongues, and were in danger of despising those who did not manifest this gift, the Apostle was quick to remind them that *every* believer in the body of Christ is a gifted individual whom the body needs to function properly.[37] "In one Spirit," he declares, all believers were "baptized into one body—Jews or Greeks, slaves or free—and all were made to drink of one Spirit."[38] The fundamental unity of Christians, established by the Holy Spirit on the basis of the death of Christ, is a unity that transcends religious heritage, economic status, and in this context, even spiritual giftedness.

In Romans Paul again returns to the issue which he had taken up in his letter to the Galatians: how do sinful men and women find complete and full acceptance by a holy and just God? Some Jewish Christians found it extremely difficult to shed the basic assumptions with which they had grown up, namely, that the Jewish religious heritage, epitomized in circumcision and strict adherence to the Jewish food laws, was necessary for salvation. We see this struggle, for instance, in the life of the Apostle Peter, who, as a believer of some years' standing, was still clearly wrestling with whether or not it was right to eat with Gentile believers.[39]

Paul's response to this particular struggle was twofold. First, he systematically laid out, for his own day and for all time, the only way that a man or a woman finds peace with God: since "all," both Jew and Gentile, "have sinned and fall short of the glory of God,"[40] then all must come to God in the identical way, namely, through faith in Christ Jesus, who was crucified for sinners. As Paul says later in the tenth chapter of Romans: "there is no distinction between Jew and Greek; the same Lord is Lord of all,

---

[37] See 1 Corinthians 12–14.
[38] 1 Corinthians 12:13.
[39] See Galatians 2:11–13.
[40] Romans 3:23.

bestowing his riches on all who call on him. For 'everyone who calls on the name of the Lord will be saved'."[41]

Then, Paul was willing to give his life for the sake of this unity created by the Spirit and take up to Jerusalem a tangible witness to that unity: a collection of money from Gentile Christian pockets for the relief of poor Jewish believers. When Paul later wrote from a prison cell in Rome to the Ephesian church that they needed to be zealous to preserve the "unity of the Spirit," the Apostle knew from real experience something of what this might cost.[42] Many years later John Calvin well expressed the heart of Paul's thinking when, in his preface to his commentary on 2 Thessalonians, he said of himself—but the words can equally apply to Paul—"my ministry ... ought to be dearer to me than my own life."[43] But Paul knew that all who love what the Spirit loves can walk no other path.

If one compares this Paul, willing to die for the Spirit's work in unifying believers, to the Saul, whom the Risen Christ transformed on the Damascus Road, what a change in temper and passion! That Saul was a religious zealot filled with hate and violence for the followers of the Lord Jesus. This Paul was now a man of love, willing to be killed for the sake of Christ and his work through the Spirit in the Church. And why the change? The Spirit who had come to indwell him was none other than the Spirit of love and a Spirit of unity. And so it is with all truly Spirit-filled men and women

---

[41] Romans 10:12–13.

[42] Ephesians 4:3.

[43] "To the distinguished Benedict Textor, Physician" in *Epistles of Paul the Apostle to the Romans and to the Thessalonians*, 385. I am indebted for this reference to Victor Shepherd, "My Ministry is Dearer to Me than Life" (Sermon, Annual Meeting of the Centre for Mentorship and Theological Reflection, at Tyndale Seminary, Toronto, June 5, 2008). This address can now be found in Victor Shepherd, *A Ministry Dearer Than Life: The Pastoral Legacy of John Calvin* (Toronto: Clements Publishing, 2009), 51–60.

9

A HIGH PNEUMATOLOGY: LEANING ON THE HOLY SPIRIT IN 2 TIMOTHY[1]

Without the Spirit of God we cannot be saved.

Irenaeus of Lyons
(*c.*130–*c.*200)

One of the ever-recurring features of human history is war. Often fed by human love of empire and desire for domination, or ethnic pride and hatred of other peoples, men go into battle to kill or be killed. Wives are widowed, young women lose their sweethearts, children their fathers, parents their sons, sisters their brothers. Yet terrible as war is, I do not believe that the Bible teaches pacifism.

When John the Baptist, for instance, was asked by some soldiers what kind of lives they should live that befit those who were repentant of their sin, John told them: "Do not extort money from anyone by threats or by false accusation, and be content with your wages."[2] Nothing is said about their leaving the army. And Paul, when dealing with the realities of political life in Romans 13, declared that the state has the right to exercise capital punishment.[3] From this text, Christian theologians from Augustine onwards

---

[1] This address was first given at the Evangelical Movement of Wales Ministers' Conference, Bala, Wales, June 18, 2008.

[2] Luke 3:14.

[3] Romans 13:1–4.

120

have argued that this implies that the use of violence by the state in self-defense is not at all illegitimate and that there is such a thing as a "just war."

And obviously in the Old Testament, war is recognized as part of the reality of living in that unique situation when God was in covenant with a nation, namely the people of Israel. For example, in Deuteronomy 20, God laid down rules on how his ancient covenant people were to conduct themselves in war. Heading the list was the command that, when they went into battle, they were to trust unconditionally in the Lord and his mighty power:

> When you go out to war against your enemies, and see horses and chariots and an army larger than your own, you shall not be afraid of them, for the Lord your God is with you, who brought you up out of the land of Egypt. And when you draw near to the battle, the priest shall come forward and speak to the people and shall say to them, "Hear, O Israel, today you are drawing near for battle against your enemies: let not your heart faint. Do not fear or panic or be in dread of them, for the Lord your God is he who goes with you to fight for you against your enemies, to give you the victory."[4]

Now, in the era of the new covenant, God's people are also engaged in a war, but this war is not one that involves earthly weapons and the battles of earthly armies, the conquest of nations and the killing of human beings. As the Lord Jesus told the Roman governor Pilate, whose rule in Judaea was supported by the military might of the Roman Imperium: "My kingdom is not of this world. If my kingdom were of this world, my servants would have been fighting, that I might not be delivered over to the Jews. But

---

[4] Deuteronomy 20:1–4 ESV.

my kingdom is not from the world."[5] Or as Paul put it: "though we walk in the flesh, we are not waging war according to the flesh."[6]

And similar to the warfare of the Old Testament, the warfare in which the church is engaged also has its rules, of which the first is identical to that which we have read in Deuteronomy: trust wholeheartedly in the Lord and his almighty power. Now, one place that such wholehearted trust is inculcated is in the first chapter of 2 Timothy.

The historical context of 2 Timothy

2 Timothy, as Gordon Fee states, is "a kind of last will and testament, a passing on of the mantle" from Paul to Timothy.[7] Paul has been arrested, probably in Asia Minor. Timothy is still in Asia Minor, in the city of Ephesus.[8] Certain Christian leaders in the Roman province of Asia, whom Paul names—Phygelus and Hermogenes—and whom he expected to have helped him, deserted him,[9] and now he is in prison in Rome.[10] He has undergone a kind of preliminary trial to determine if there is enough evidence to take him to a full trial.[11] This first trial may well have been presided over by Ophonius Tigellinus (d.69), the notorious and vicious head of the Praetorian Guard. Paul refers to his coming through this first trial as having been "rescued from the lion's mouth."[12] At this defense, though, Paul expected to have been supported by some of the believers in Rome, but they too apparently failed

---

[5] John 18:36 ESV.

[6] 2 Corinthians 10:3 ESV.

[7] *1 and 2 Timothy, Titus* (Rev. ed.; San Francisco: Harper & Row, 1988), xxv.

[8] 2 Timothy 1:16–18; 4:19.

[9] 2 Timothy 1:15.

[10] 2 Timothy 1:16–17; 2:9.

[11] 2 Timothy 4:16.

[12] 2 Timothy 4:17.

him.[13]

Although he has survived this first trial, Paul is quite certain of what will be the final outcome of the trial process: his condemnation and death.[14] He thus urges Timothy to come as fast as he can to Rome, which means sailing from Ephesus before the winter storms make navigating the Mediterranean dangerous, something Paul the seasoned traveler of the Mediterranean knows all too well.[15] But in case Timothy does not reach Rome in time before Paul's execution, Paul uses the written word in place of the spoken word to urge Timothy to guard the gospel from theological error, to stay true to what he has been taught and to be faithful in preaching the Word.[16]

The latter admonitions are also necessary because Paul is deeply concerned about a problem in the church at Ephesus that is as equally serious a problem as persecution by the Roman state. There are leaders in the house churches of Ephesus who have fallen into grave error. In a departure from his normal method of dealing with theological errorists, Paul names two of these leaders: Hymenaeus and Philetus.[17] The teaching of these men was not at all promoting the spiritual health of the believers in Ephesus. On the contrary, Paul could only liken their teaching to "gangrene" for it had a dangerous tendency to spread falsehood to believers just as gangrene infects and eats up neighboring tissue.[18]

---

[13] 2 Timothy 4:16. Are these the brothers and sister Paul names in 2 Timothy 4:21?

[14] 2 Timothy 4:6–8.

[15] 2 Timothy 4:9, 21. For one of Paul's voyages on the Mediterranean that involved a shipwreck, see Acts 27–28. In 2 Corinthians 11:25–26 Paul mentions being in danger while on the sea and specifically being shipwrecked three times, on one occasion spending "a night and a day" adrift at sea.

[16] 2 Timothy 1:14; 3:14–15; 4:2.

[17] 2 Timothy 2:17. See also 1 Timothy 1:18–20.

[18] J.N.D. Kelly, *A Commentary on The Pastoral Epistles: Timothy I & II, and Titus* (1960 ed.; repr. Peabody: Hendrickson Publishers, 1987), 184; Philip H. Towner, *The Letters to Timothy and Titus* (Grand Rapids/Cambridge: Wm. B. Eerdmans, 2006), 525.

What were they teaching? Paul mentions only one specific: the denial of the bodily resurrection.[19] Hymenaeus and Philetus probably shared a common Greek conviction that only the soul was of true value and the body was to be shed at death like a useless shell.[20] If so, their teaching seems to have anticipated the errors of the Gnostic of the second century who despised the body and refused to believe it could be included in redemption.[21]

In the final letter of the Puritan theologian John Owen before his death on August 24, 1683, he told a close friend, Charles Fleetwood, "I am leaving the ship of the church in a storm," a reference to the persecution that Dissenters like him were experiencing at the time from the English state.[22] Given what we have just seen with regard to the historical context of 2 Timothy, Paul could well have said the same thing to Timothy. Paul and the church in Ephesus were facing enemies from without the church and enemies from within. The situation clearly called for courage, stalwart leadership and a wise head.

A high pneumatology

It is no surprise, therefore, to find the Apostle emphasizing right at the beginning of 2 Timothy, in what we designate as chapter 1, that the only way in which Timothy can hope to stand firm is through the power of the Holy Spirit. For Paul, ultimately only the Spirit of God can make a person adequate for all the challenges of

---

[19] 2 Timothy 2:17–18. For other probable reflections on these false teachers, see: 2 Timothy 2:14 and 16, which mentions quarreling about words and "irreverent babble" and 2 Timothy 2:23, which refers to "foolish, ignorant controversies. 2 Timothy 3:1–9 may also refer to these men. On the "irreverent babble," see also 1 Timothy 6:20–21.

[20] For a different theological reconstruction of the error in view here, see Towner, *Letters to Timothy and Titus*, 526–529.

[21] Another element of the errors at Ephesus, the rejection of marriage (1 Timothy 4:1–3), also anticipates second-century Gnosticism.

[22] *The Correspondence of John Owen*, ed. Peter Toon (Cambridge: James Clarke, 1970), 174.

the Christian life, especially those of leadership in the Church.[23]

The structure of the first eighteen verses of the letter clearly highlights this emphasis that Paul wishes to make with regard to the Holy Spirit. In common with his normal pattern at the outset of a letter, Paul has a greeting[24] followed by a thanksgiving. [25] In this case, the thanksgiving leads directly into an admonition to Timothy to use his Spirit-endowed gift or gifts and not give way to fear.[26] Closing the passage is a second admonition about the indwelling Spirit: Timothy is to guard the faith "by the Holy Spirit who dwells within us."[27] Also tying together the passage is the word "ashamed" (*epaischynomai*): Timothy is to rely on the Spirit's power so that he will not be ashamed of the gospel—by implication, Paul is doing so and so is not ashamed—Onesiphorus, again by implication, is held up as an example of one who also relied on the Spirit's power and so was not ashamed.[28]

In 2 Timothy 1:6 Paul begins from the basic fact that Timothy is a genuine believer. As such, Paul can assume he has at least one gift of the Spirit for service in the Body of Christ.[29] Although the Apostle does not name Timothy's gift explicitly, it clearly had to do with preaching and leadership in the local church, otherwise Paul's later admonitions to Timothy to teach those in error with gentleness and to preach the Word make no sense.[30] Paul specifically urges Timothy to "fan into flame" his spiritual gift. The verb

---

[23] For Paul's teaching on the Holy Spirit, see Gordon D. Fee, *God's Empowering Presence: The Holy Spirit in the Letters of Paul* (Peabody: Hendrickson Publishers, 1994).

[24] 2 Timothy 1:1–2.

[25] 2 Timothy 1:3–5.

[26] 2 Timothy 1:6–7.

[27] 2 Timothy 1:14.

[28] 2 Timothy 1:8, 12, 16.

[29] See Paul's argument in 1 Corinthians 12.

[30] See, for example, Paul's words in 2 Timothy 2:24–26; 4:1–2. Towner argues that the "gift of God" in view here is the Spirit himself. See Towner, *Letters to Timothy and Titus*, 457–460.

"fan into flame" Paul uses here does not imply that Timothy has so neglected his gift that it has to be fanned into flame from dying embers. Rather, Paul is likening Timothy's gift to a fire which needs constant stirring to be kept at full flame. Paul is concerned that given the dangers of persecution and heresy Timothy may give way to timidity and not be as zealous in the exercise of his spiritual gift as he could be.

Paul can exhort Timothy to employ his gifts because, as he now goes on to state in verse 7, the source of these gifts is not Timothy's own inner resources but the Holy Spirit, whom God has given—"a spirit not of fear but of power and love and self-control." The word translated "fear" here, or "timidity" as some translations have it,[31] actually has the connotation of "cowardice" and was often used in battle accounts. In the words of Gordon Fee, it describes "the terror that overtakes the fearful in extreme difficulties."[32] In other words, Paul is reminding Timothy that the One who has gifted him for ministry, namely the Spirit, is not One who will lead him to neglect his gift and run away from his responsibilities.

The Holy Spirit whom God has given to his children is characterized by three traits. First, he is a Spirit of power, one who fills believers with power to live for God and his glory, no matter the circumstances. This empowering comes not from the believer's own resources, but lies in the inexhaustible strength of the divine Holy Spirit. The Scriptures frequently mention the Spirit as a Spirit of empowerment.[33] In Acts 6, for instance, Stephen is described as a man "full of grace and power," whose words, when he bore witness to Christ, were irresistible because of "the

---

[31] The KJV and ESV have "fear," while the NIV and NASB have "timidity."

[32] *1 and 2 Timothy, Titus*, 177.

[33] Consider, in addition to the texts discussed below, Zechariah 4:6–9; Acts 10:38; Philippians 1:19; Ephesians 3:16.

wisdom and the Spirit" with which he spoke.[34] Again, in 1 Thessalonians 1:4–5, Paul is confident that the Thessalonian believers are enrolled among God's chosen people, because when he was preaching the gospel to them he was conscious that the Spirit was driving home the truth of his words to them and bringing them under divine conviction. The Spirit's power quickened the Apostle's words and applied them to hearts of his audience. Similarly in Romans 15:19, Paul defines his ministry as one which does not deal with mere form and ritual, but results in powerful Spirit-wrought conversions.[35] These three texts reveal the biblical emphasis that genuine ministry is accomplished not by human strength, but through the powerful, empowering work of the Spirit. So, it is no surprise that when Paul comes to exhort Timothy to fulfill his ministry, he stresses the urgent need for Timothy to find his source of strength in the Spirit of God.

Then, the Spirit is a Spirit of love, One who promotes "self-sacrificing, affectionate service" to others.[36] Again, this connection between the Spirit and love is characteristically Pauline. One need only think of Galatians 5:22 where Paul lists the fruit of the Spirit, the solid evidence of the Spirit's indwelling presence, and love heads the list and, from one perspective, defines all of the other characteristics. It will take love to truly deal with those who are promoting error. Look at the way Paul spells this out in 2 Timothy 2:24–26. The Christian leader—"the Lord's servant"—must be able to engage those in error with firmness—he is to teach and correct—but it must be done with kindness, patience, and gentleness. He also needs to pray for the opponents of the truth

---

[34] Acts 6:8, 10.

[35] Clark Pinnock, "The Concept of Spirit in the Epistles of Paul" (Unpublished Ph.D. Thesis, Manchester, 1963), 126. Unlike Clark Pinnock's more recent work, this thesis is an admirable exploration of Pauline pneumatology. See also 1 Corinthians 4:20.

[36] Kelly, *Pastoral Epistles*, 160.

that God might give them an opportunity to repent and embrace the truth.

Finally, Paul states that the Spirit is a Spirit of "self-control." The Greek word at this point—*sōphronismos*—has taken some commentators by surprise, for it is a term that is regularly used by Hellenistic manuals of moral behavior and the word itself occurs nowhere else in the New Testament, although various cognate words do appear in the Pastoral Epistles.[37] However, the surrounding context is extremely Pauline in emphasis: none of the terms listed in verse 7 are regarded as the result of mere human effort, but all are the fruit of the Spirit. Here, in this third trait Paul is emphasizing that the Spirit is One who enables the believer to make sober judgments and to keep his head in fearful situations—both of which were especially appropriate for Timothy given his situation.

What we have here then is a deep appreciation of the believer's and the church's vital need for the Spirit to fulfill the task of ministry. Without his power, love, and self-control, all is vain. Like Timothy, believers in every age must trust in the Spirit's power as they seek to live lives that glorify God. In other words, Paul is arguing in a fashion similar to what was said in Deuteronomy 20: in the context of spiritual warfare, the believer's trust must be in the Lord, the Holy Spirit. If this is so, what we have here then is evidence of a high pneumatology, in which the Spirit is implicitly lauded as God, for the believer's hope and confidence is never directed to any but God alone.

The Spirit of the crucified and risen Lord

In view of the spiritual resources that the Spirit has given Timothy, Paul now urges his dear friend "not [to] be ashamed of the

---

[37] See Kelly, *Pastoral Epistles*, 160.

testimony about our Lord, nor of me his prisoner, but share in suffering for the gospel by the power of God."[38] The key word here is "power." Paul has just told Timothy that he can have confidence in using his gift for God since the One indwelling him, who is the source of this gift, is a Spirit of power. Trust in the Spirit's power to face the problems of persecution and heresy. Now, Paul calls upon Timothy to be loyal to both the Lord Jesus and to himself, the Lord's prisoner. It is an appeal which, if Timothy responds positively, will inevitably involve him in humiliation and suffering. But this humiliation and suffering can be borne if Timothy relies on "the power of God" that is the power which God gives through his Spirit.

It is absolutely vital to note that here we have a paradox that Paul enunciates in greater detail elsewhere in his letters: namely, that the Spirit's power does not eliminate suffering and weakness—rather it manifests itself *in* weakness. Without agreeing with all that James D.G. Dunn has written, surely he is right when he states that, for Paul:

> weakness does not hinder or prevent the manifestation of power; on the contrary it is the necessary presupposition of power, the place wherein and the means whereby divine power is revealed ... power does not drive out weakness; on the contrary, it only comes to its full strength in and through weakness.[39]

Verses 9–10 then provide a further reflection on the power of God. Timothy can wholly rely on the Spirit's power, for it was that power which was at work in the crucified Christ, "rendering death

---

[38] 2 Timothy 1:8 ESV.
[39] *Jesus and the Spirit* (London: SCM Press Ltd., 1975), 329.

ineffectual"[40] and revealing life and immortality. Implicit in the statements of these two verses is the paradox just noted: God's most powerful work, the salvific work of the cross, was accomplished through the utter frailty of his Son. Paul puts it this way in 2 Corinthians 13:4, Christ "was crucified in weakness." Yet, in the midst of the Son's weakness, the Holy Spirit was powerfully at work, so that Paul can also say in 1 Corinthians 1:23–24 that Christ crucified is for "those who are called, both Jews and Greeks, … the power of God."[41] Suffering and weakness by no means imply the absence of God's Spirit. On the contrary, they are *the medium* in which the Spirit delights to work. Since the Spirit indwelling believers is the Spirit of the crucified Christ, the same pattern can be seen to be at work in believers: the power of the Spirit displayed in the midst of human weakness.

Onesiphorus, a Spirit-filled man

Paul has urged Timothy not to be ashamed of the gospel and states that he himself, solely because of grace and the Spirit's power,[42] is not ashamed.[43] And to further encourage Timothy to trust in the Spirit's power he gives the example of Onesiphorus. Unlike Phygelus and Hermogenes, elders probably in the churches of Asia, who were ashamed to be associated with Paul the "criminal,"[44] Onesiphorus "was not ashamed of [Paul's] chains." Unlike his earlier imprisonment in Rome, when he lived under house arrest in a locale known to many,[45] Paul appears to have been imprisoned in a cell not easily found, for Onesiphorus had to expend

---

[40] Fee, *1 and 2 Timothy, Titus*, 180.

[41] ESV.

[42] 2 Timothy 1:9.

[43] 2 Timothy 1:12.

[44] 2 Timothy 1:15; 2:9.

[45] Acts 28:30.

much energy in the search for the whereabouts of the Apostle.[46] And when he found Paul, he was not content with a single visit. But again and again he visited Paul, risking arrest and imprisonment with the Christian leader. But Onesiphorus was "not ashamed."[47] Why? From the verses that precede—which we have already looked at—one can only conclude that Onesiphorus' courage was because of the power of the indwelling Spirit. Onesiphorus stands as a model of the Spirit-filled, Spirit-empowered man.

Notice further that Paul is not ashamed to own that Onesiphorus refreshed him. At a basic level, such refreshment would have involved food and other means of practical help.[48] But at a deeper level it would have entailed the Spirit-given joys of Christian fellowship. As Dietrich Bonhoeffer (1906–1945) has rightly noted in his spiritual classic *Life Together*: "The physical presence of other Christians is a source of incomparable joy and strength to the believer."[49] In fact, as has been noted above, a key reason for the writing of 2 Timothy was Paul's desire to have Timothy come to Rome to see before him before he leaves this world. Twice near the end of the letter he reiterates this desire: "Do your best to come to me soon"—"Do your best to come before winter."[50]

Did Timothy go? Did he heed Paul's admonition and overcome any fears of associating with Paul by the Spirit's power? We do not know the answer for sure, but there is a tantalizing verse at the close of the Book of Hebrews, where the anonymous author

---

[46] 2 Timothy 1:17.

[47] 2 Timothy 1:16.

[48] Towner, *Letters to Timothy and Titus*, 483.

[49] *Life Together*, trans. John W. Doberstein (1954 ed.; repr. New York: HarperCollins Publishers, n.d.), 19.

[50] 2 Timothy 4:9, 21 ESV.

tells his readers that "our brother Timothy has been released."[51] It appears quite likely that Timothy, empowered by the Spirit, did indeed go to Rome, and there experienced imprisonment for the sake of the gospel. And so, he showed himself a true disciple of the Lord Jesus and his friend and mentor, Paul.

---

[51] Hebrews 13:23.

10
C.H. Spurgeon and the power of the Holy Spirit

"The Holy Spirit always keeps sweet company with Jesus Christ"

C.H. Spurgeon (1834–1892)

In the previous chapter we have noted the way that Paul, in his final canonical letter, 2 Timothy, urges Timothy to rely on the power of the Holy Spirit. An excellent case-study of a Christian who followed Paul's advice was Charles Haddon Spurgeon (1834–1892). Spurgeon was born into a godly home in the heart of rural Essex on June 19, 1834. Spurgeon's forebears originally came from the Netherlands, which they had left in the sixteenth century due to religious persecution. Both Spurgeon's father, John Spurgeon (1811–1902), and his grandfather, James Spurgeon (1776–1864), were Congregationalist preachers, and it was during an extended stay over a number of years in the home of his grandfather that Spurgeon was first exposed to the writings of the Puritans. James Spurgeon was the pastor of the Congregational church in the village of Stambourne in the heart of rural Essex. Here in the parsonage the young Spurgeon discovered a library of Puritan folios. They had been collected by Henry Havers (1620–*c*.1712), who had pastored the Stambourne church after his ejection from the Church of England in 1662 when he refused to comply with the Act of Uniformity.

Despite Spurgeon's tender years and the fact that as a young child he found it very difficult to lift these large and weighty

Puritan volumes, he would later write that as a boy he was never happier than when in the company of these Puritan authors.[1] After his conversion in January of 1850, Spurgeon collected original Puritan editions with zest and fervour. Not content with reading the works of these seventeenth-century authors himself, he never ceased to recommend them to his fellow believers. For instance, in a sermon entitled "Paul—His Cloak and His Books," which Spurgeon preached in November of 1863, he urged his hearers to follow the Apostle Paul's example and to read good books:

> Renounce as much as you will all light literature, but study as much as possible sound theological works, especially the Puritanic writers, and expositions of the Bible. We are quite persuaded that the very best way for you to be spending your leisure, is to be either reading or praying.[2]

Spurgeon was especially convinced that wide exposure to the Puritans was a vital part of ministerial training. Thus, at his Pastor's College, which was founded in 1856, the theology that was taught was rooted in the Puritans. In defence of this methodology, Spurgeon said:

> We are old-fashioned enough to prefer Manton to Maurice, Charnock to Robertson, and Owen to Voysey. Both our experience and our reading of the Scriptures confirm us in the belief of the unfashionable doctrines of grace; and among us, upon those grand fundamentals, there is no uncertain sound.[3]

---

[1] *C.H. Spurgeon: The Early Years 1834–1859* (London: The Banner of Truth Trust, 1962), 11.

[2] *The Metropolitan Tabernacle Pulpit* (London: Passmore and Alabaster, 1864), 9:668.

[3] *Early Years*, 387.

Indeed, Spurgeon was rightly convinced that it was commitment to these doctrines that had preserved the Baptist denomination over the centuries.[4]

Spurgeon—heir of the Puritan interest in the Holy Spirit

Now, one of the distinctive marks of Puritan theology is its emphasis on the person and work of the Holy Spirit. Numerous authors over the years have commented on this distinct characteristic. B.B. Warfield, Spurgeon's younger contemporary, noted eight years after Spurgeon's death that:

> The developed doctrine of the work of the Holy Spirit is an exclusively Reformation doctrine, and more particularly a Reformed doctrine, and more particularly still a Puritan doctrine... Puritan thought was almost entirely occupied with loving study of the work of the Holy Spirit, and found its highest expression in dogmatico-practical expositions of the several aspects of it.[5]

More recently, Richard F. Lovelace has reiterated Warfield's judgment and maintained that "the English Puritans (particularly John Owen and Richard Sibbes) have given us the most profound and extensive biblical-theological studies of the ministry of the Holy Spirit which exist in any language."[6] Given Spurgeon's love for and constant study of the Puritans, it is not at all surprising that this leading characteristic of Puritanism is also reproduced in Spurgeon's sermons and writings. In fact, so extensive is the material by Spurgeon on the person and work of the Spirit that it

---

[4] *Early Years*, 174.

[5] "Introductory Note" to Abraham Kuyper, *The Work of the Holy Spirit*, trans. Henri de Vries (1900 ed.; repr. Grand Rapids: Wm. B. Eerdmans, 1956), xxxiii, xxviii.

[6] *Dynamics of Spiritual Life. An Evangelical Theology of Renewal* (Downers Grove: InterVarsity Press, 1979), 120.

would take a monograph devoted to the subject to do real justice to his teaching on the Holy Spirit. What follows, though, has a much more modest goal, namely, to provide an introduction to the Baptist preacher's doctrine of the Holy Spirit by focusing on his conviction that "where the Spirit of God is, there is power."[7]

The vital necessity of the Holy Spirit

During 1859, when a powerful revival swept through much of Great Britain, Spurgeon preached a series of sermons on what are sometimes referred to as "the five points of Calvinism." He was firmly convinced that the proclamation of these doctrines would help further the revival that was then underway.[8] One of these sermons, entitled "The Necessity of the Spirit's Work," begins by sketching the Biblical teaching on men and women outside of Christ: they are dead in sin, "utterly and entirely averse to everything that is good and right," totally unwilling to come to Christ.[9] Only the Spirit, Spurgeon avers, can remedy this situation; he alone can change the will, "correct the bias of the heart," set men and women on the right road and "give [them] strength to run in it."[10]

When Spurgeon turns to examine the means by which the Spirit brings men and women to Christ—for instance, the preaching of the Word—and the means by which he takes them on to maturity—for example, baptism and the Lord's Supper—he finds that all of these means are completely inadequate unless the Spirit deigns to use them.[11] Indeed, Spurgeon stresses, until the Spirit

---

[7] "The Holy Ghost the Need of the Age," *The Metropolitan Tabernacle Pulpit* (London: Passmore and Alabaster, 1888), 33:146.

[8] Eric W. Hayden, *Spurgeon on Revival. A Biblical and Theological Approach* (Grand Rapids: Zondervan, 1962), 85.

[9] *The New Park Street Pulpit* (London: Passmore and Alabaster, 1860), 5:210.

[10] *The New Park Street Pulpit*, 5:210.

[11] *The New Park Street Pulpit*, 5:210–12.

calls the unbeliever out of darkness into the light of God's kingdom, his or her "election is a dead letter."[12] Likewise, the redemption accomplished by the Lord Jesus is of no avail, until the Spirit applies Christ's redemptive work to the soul.

> Christ's blood and righteousness are like wine stored in the wine-vat; but we cannot get thereat. The Holy Spirit dips our vessel into this precious wine, and then we drink; but without the Spirit we must die and perish just as much, though the Father elect and the Son redeem, as though the Father had never elected, and though the Son had never bought us with his blood. The Spirit is absolutely necessary. Without him neither the works of the Father, nor of the Son, are of any avail to us.[13]

Spurgeon concludes this sermon by stressing that the vital necessity of the Spirit's work in the believer does not come to an end at conversion; for "the acceptable acts of the Christian's life, cannot be performed without the Spirit."[14] Four years later, preaching on Acts 2:1–4, Spurgeon again emphasized "how absolutely necessary is the presence and power of the Holy Spirit."

> It is not possible for us to promote the glory of God or to bless the souls of men, unless the Holy Ghost shall be in us and with us. Those who were assembled on that memorable day of Pentecost, were all men of prayer and faith; but even these precious gifts are only available when the celestial fire sets them on a blaze. ... [E]ven these favoured and honoured saints can do nothing without the breath of God the Holy Ghost. ... [I]f so it was with them, much more must it be the case with us. Let us

---

12 *The New Park Street Pulpit*, 5:212.
13 *The New Park Street Pulpit*, 5:213.
14 *The New Park Street Pulpit*, 5:215.

beware of trusting to our well-adjusted machineries of committees and schemes; let us be jealous of all reliance upon our own mental faculties or religious vigour; let us be careful that we do not look too much to our leading preachers and evangelists, for if we put any of these in the place of the Divine Spirit, we shall err most fatally.[15]

This absolute need of the Spirit on the part of the church and of the individual believer is a constant refrain in Spurgeon's sermons and writings over the next twenty-nine years till his death in 1892. For instance, in a sermon preached in 1864 on "The Superlative Excellence of the Holy Spirit," he challenges his hearers:

Do not say that we want money; we shall have it soon enough when the Spirit touches men's hearts. Do not say that we want buildings, churches, edifices; all these may be very well in subserviency, but the main want of the Church is the Spirit, and men into whom the Spirit may be poured.[16]

Thus, Spurgeon was constrained to pray in the middle of the sermon: "Come, Holy Spirit, come, we can do nothing without thee; but if we have thy wind, we spread our sail, and speed onward towards glory."[17]

Keeping in step with the Spirit

The church's need of the Spirit carries with it certain responsibilities, and Spurgeon, like his beloved Puritans, was not slow to point these out. In "The Superlative Excellence of the Holy Spirit," Spurgeon emphasizes that the Spirit must be treated with

---

[15] "Pentecost," *The Metropolitan Tabernacle Pulpit*, 9:289.
[16] *The Metropolitan Tabernacle Pulpit* (London: Passmore and Alabaster, 1865), 10:337.
[17] *The Metropolitan Tabernacle Pulpit*, 10:336.

"deep awe and reverence." Believers must be careful not to grieve him or provoke him to anger through sin. Moreover, if "the Holy Spirit be indeed so mighty, let us do nothing without him; let us begin no project, and carry on no enterprise, and conclude no transaction, without imploring his blessing."[18]

In a later sermon, entitled "The Paraclete," which was preached in 1872, Spurgeon reminded his audience that if they truly considered the Spirit to be their "sole force," then they ought to: "Love the Spirit, worship the Spirit, trust the Spirit, obey the Spirit, and, as a church, cry mightily to the Spirit. Beseech him to let his mighty power be known and felt among you."[19] And putting his own advice into practice, Spurgeon went on to cry: "Come, Holy Spirit now! Thou art with us, but come with power and let us feel thy sacred might!"[20]

Spurgeon was all too aware of the consequences of failing to heed such advice. In a sermon preached two years before "The Paraclete," the Baptist preacher laid before the congregation of the Metropolitan Tabernacle what he called "A Most Needful Prayer Concerning the Holy Spirit." His text was the prayer of David in Psalm 51:11: "Cast me not away from thy presence; and take not thy Holy Spirit from me." After a personal confession, in which Spurgeon declared that he "would sooner die a thousand times, than lose the helpful presence of the Holy Ghost," he used a vivid illustration, fresh in the minds of his hearers, to depict the church from which the Spirit has departed. On the other side of the English Channel the Franco-Prussian War was raging, and, as Spurgeon preached, the war was going badly for the French, who would suffer a humiliating defeat at the hands of the Prussians at

---

[18] *The Metropolitan Tabernacle Pulpit*, 10:338.

[19] *The Metropolitan Tabernacle Pulpit* (London: Passmore and Alabaster, 1873), 18:564.

[20] *The Metropolitan Tabernacle Pulpit*, 18:564.

the end of that year. "Any church from which the Spirit has departed," Spurgeon declared,

> becomes very like that great empire with whose military glory the world was dazzled, and whose strength made the nations tremble.
>
> France, mistress of arms, queen of beauty, arbiter of politics, how soon has she fallen! ... The nation once so great now lies bleeding at her victor's feet, pitied of us all none the less because her folly continues the useless fight. Just so have we seen it in churches; may we never so see it here.[21]

Spurgeon turns to the geography of Egypt to drive his point home even further. Areas of land in Egypt which were once fertile because of life-giving irrigation canals drawn from the Nile River are now desert simply because these canals have been allowed to lapse into disuse. So it is with churches, Spurgeon emphasizes. Churches "irrigated by the Spirit," he declared, "once produced rich harvests of souls; left of the Spirit the sand of the world has covered them, and where once all was green and beautiful there is nothing but the former howling wilderness."[22]

Sticking with Egypt for a further illustration, Spurgeon takes up an aspect of the history of that land. The nineteenth century witnessed the systematic ransacking of the Egyptian pyramids by European archaeologists and explorers. Prominent amongst the treasures found in these pyramids were the mummified bodies of the Pharaohs. Spurgeon clearly has little sympathy with the removal of these bodies of the ancient Egyptian kings. Their discovery and exposure to "every vulgar eye" awakens in Spurgeon

---

[21] *The Metropolitan Tabernacle Pulpit* (London: Passmore and Alabaster, 1871), 16:562.
[22] *The Metropolitan Tabernacle Pulpit*, 16:563.

"melancholy reflections." These poor mummies, "once a Pharaoh whose voice could shake a nation and devastate continents," are now mere objects for a museum. And now Spurgeon draws the comparison with the local church:

> [A]live by the divine indwelling, God gives it royalty, and makes it a king and priest unto himself among the sons of men; its influence is felt further than it dreams; the world trembles at it, for it is fair as the sun, clear as the moon, and terrible as an army with banners; but when the Spirit of God is departed, what remains but its old records, ancient creeds, title-deeds, traditions, histories and memories? it is in fact a mummy of a church rather than a church of God, and it is better fitted to be looked at by antiquarians than to be treated as an existent agency.[23]

The Holy Spirit and the pastor

Spurgeon was also insistent that those who pastor and preach be continually conscious of their deep need of the Spirit of God. At his Pastor's College he particularly sought to inculcate in the minds and hearts of the students such a consciousness. The College had begun in 1856 with one student, Thomas W. Medhurst (1834–1917). By 1877, there were 110 men attending the college full-time.[24] That same year Spurgeon published his *Second Series of Lectures to My Students*, a series of addresses that he had regularly given at the college on Friday afternoons. In the first volume of lectures, which he admitted were more akin to sermons than lectures, Spurgeon had explored the pastor's life as it relates to his walk with God, his preaching, and his health. In this second book

---

[23] *The Metropolitan Tabernacle Pulpit*, 16:563.

[24] For information regarding the Pastor's College, see M. Nicholls, "Charles Haddon Spurgeon, Educationalist," *The Baptist Quarterly* 31 (1985–1986): 384–401; 32 (1987–1988), 73–94.

Spurgeon treated, amongst other things, the pastor's relationship to the Holy Spirit.

After some initial remarks on the reality of the Spirit's existence, Spurgeon comes to what he describes in no uncertain terms as "the core of our subject." For those who are ministers, he solemnly declares:

> [T]he Holy Spirit is absolutely essential. Without Him our office is a mere name. We claim no priesthood over and above that which belongs to every child of God; but we are the successors of those who, in olden times, were moved of God to declare His word, to testify against transgression, and to lead His cause. Unless we have the spirit of the prophets resting upon us, the mantle which we wear is nothing but a rough garment to deceive. We ought to be driven forth with abhorrence from the society of honest men for daring to speak in the name of the Lord if the Spirit of God rests not upon us.[25]

In what areas, Spurgeon goes on to ask, should those in pastoral ministry especially seek the help of the Spirit? Spurgeon proceeds to answer this question with a list of eight areas in which the Spirit's aid is vital. Quoting John 16:13, a favourite passage of his when it came to discussing the work of the Spirit, Spurgeon states that the Spirit is the "Spirit of knowledge." He opens up the Scriptures, and takes especial delight in focusing the pastor's attention on "the centre of our testimony," the person and work of the Lord Jesus.[26]

---

[25] "The Holy Spirit in Connection with our Ministry" in *Lectures to My Students* (London/Edinburgh: Marshall, Morgan & Scott, 1954), 186–187.

[26] "The Holy Spirit in Connection with our Ministry" in *Lectures to My Students*, 188–189.

The Spirit is also the "Spirit of wisdom," the one who gives the ability to rightly apply the knowledge obtained from the study of Scripture and to preach with balance. For instance, Spurgeon is convinced that:

> [M]any brethren who preach human responsibility deliver themselves in so legal a manner as to disgust all those who love the doctrines of grace. On the other hand, I fear that many have preached the sovereignty of God in such a way as to drive all persons who believe in man's free agency entirely away from the Calvinistic side. We should not hide truth for a moment, but we should have wisdom so to preach it that there shall be no needless jarring or offending.[27]

Then the Spirit is needed to give fluency of speech and freedom in preaching. Comparing the Spirit to the live coal from the altar in the vision of the prophet Isaiah (Isaiah 6:6), Spurgeon states, "Oh, how gloriously a man speaks when his lips are blistered with the live coal from the altar—feeling the burning power of the truth, not only in his inmost soul, but on the very lip with which he is speaking!"[28]

The Spirit's fourth aid in preaching is as "an anointing oil" on the preacher as he preaches, that is, enabling his mind and heart to be wrapped up in the subject of the sermon.[29] In a sermon that Spurgeon preached on Haggai 2:4-5 in September of 1886, the London Baptist made a similar point:

---

[27] "The Holy Spirit in Connection with our Ministry" in *Lectures to My Students*, 190.

[28] "The Holy Spirit in Connection with our Ministry" in *Lectures to My Students*, 191.

[29] "The Holy Spirit in Connection with our Ministry" in *Lectures to My Students*, 192–194.

Oh that the prayers of God's people would always go up for God's ministers, that they may speak with a divine power and influence which none shall be able to gainsay! We look too much for clever men; we seek out fluent and flowery speakers; we sigh for men cultured and trained in all the knowledge of the heathen: nay, but if we sought more for unction, for divine authority, and for that power which doth hedge about the man of God, how much wiser should we be! Oh, that all of us who profess to preach the Gospel would learn to speak in entire dependence upon the direction of the Holy Spirit, not daring to utter our own words, but even trembling lest we should do so, and committing ourselves to that secret influence without which nothing will be powerful upon the conscience or converting to the heart. Know ye not the difference between the power that cometh of human oratory, and that which cometh by the divine energy which speaks so to the heart that men cannot resist it? We have forgotten this too much. It were better to speak six words in the power of the Holy Ghost than to preach seventy years of sermons without the Spirit. He who rested on those who have gone to their reward in heaven can rest this day upon ministers and bless our evangelists, if we will but seek it of him. Let us cease to grieve the Spirit of God, and look to him for help to the faithful ministers who are yet spared to us.[30]

A final way in which the Spirit helps in preaching is to produce effects in those who listen:

---

[30] "The Abiding of the Spirit the Glory of the Church" (*The Metropolitan Tabernacle Pulpit* [London: Passmore and Alabaster, 1887], 32:481ff.). My attention was drawn to this text by David K. Straub, "Charles Haddon Spurgeon and 'Spirit-Anointed' Preaching" (Unpublished paper, The C.H. Spurgeon Pastors' Conference, August 10–12, 1995, William Jewel College, Liberty, Missouri), 1–2.

> Miracles of grace must be the seals of our ministry; who
> can bestow them but the Spirit of God? Convert a soul
> without the Spirit of God! Why, you cannot even make a
> fly, much less create a new heart and a right spirit. ...
> Therefore, with strong crying and tears, wait upon Him
> from day to day.[31]

Little wonder, Spurgeon comments, that the root cause of many useless ministries lies in the "lack of distinctly recognizing the power of the Holy Ghost."[32]

Remarkable instances

A remarkable illustration of Spurgeon's own dependence upon the Spirit in the pulpit occurs in his *Autobiography*. Discussing instances of striking conversions under his preaching ministry, he relates that on one occasion he deliberately pointed to a man in the congregation and said:

> "There is a man sitting there, who is a shoemaker; he
> keeps his shop open on Sundays, it was open last Sabbath
> morning, he took ninepence, and there was fourpence
> profit out of it; his soul is sold to Satan for fourpence!"
> A city missionary, when going his rounds, met with this
> man, and seeing that he was reading one of my sermons,
> he asked the question, "Do you know Mr. Spurgeon?"
> "Yes," replied the man, "I have every reason to know
> him, I have been to hear him; and, under his preaching,
> by God's grace I have become a new creature in Christ
> Jesus. Shall I tell you how it happened? I went to the Mu-
> sic Hall, and took my seat in the middle of the place; Mr.
> Spurgeon looked at me as if he knew me, and in his ser-
> mon he pointed to me, and told the congregation that I

---

[31] "The Holy Spirit in Connection with our Ministry" in *Lectures to My Students*, 195.

[32] "The Holy Spirit in Connection with our Ministry" in *Lectures to My Students*, 195.

was a shoemaker, and that I kept my shop open on Sundays; and I did, sir. I should not have minded that; but he also said that I took ninepence the Sunday before, and there was fourpence profit out of it. I did take ninepence that day, and fourpence was just the profit; but how he should know that, I could not tell. Then it struck me that it was God who had spoken to my soul through him, so I shut up my shop the next Sunday. At first, I was afraid to go again to hear him, lest he should tell the people more about me; but afterwards I went, and the Lord met with me, and saved my soul.[33]

Spurgeon went on to say that there were as "many as a dozen similar cases" in which he

pointed at somebody in the hall without having the slightest knowledge of the person, or any idea that what I said was right, except that I believed I was moved by the Spirit to say it; and so striking has been my description, that the persons have gone away, and said to their friends, "Come, see a man that told me all things that ever I did; beyond a doubt, he must have been sent of God to my soul , or else he could not have described me so exactly."[34]

Now, what is so significant about these extraordinary instances in the life of Spurgeon is that he did not make a "ministry" out of them as some would do today. They were obviously out of the norm, but Spurgeon mentions them primarily to exalt the grace of God in the salvation of sinners.

---

[33] *C.H. Spurgeon's Autobiography* (London: Passmore and Alabaster, 1899), II, 226–227.

[34] *C.H. Spurgeon's Autobiography*, II, 227. For other examples, see Ernest W. Bacon, *Spurgeon: Heir of the Puritans* (London: George Allen & Unwin Ltd., 1967), 150.

Further on the Holy Spirit and the pastor

The work of the ministry, though, contains more than preaching and its preparation in the study. There is also the important matter of prayer. Central to the minister's life is "praying in the Holy Spirit," and, Spurgeon rightly advises, "that minister who does not think so had better escape from his ministry."[35] But to maintain this life of communion with God the minister needs "secret oil to be poured upon the sacred fire of [his] heart's devotion;" he wants "again and again [to be] visited by the Spirit of grace and supplications" (cf. Zechariah 12:10).[36] Then, the minister also needs the Spirit to walk in holiness in every area of his life and to keep himself "unspotted from the world."[37] Finally, those in pastoral ministry have much need of discernment in their dealings with men and women, and here again the Spirit is absolutely necessary, "for He knows the minds of men as He knows the mind of God."[38]

Spurgeon was well aware that this list of ways in which the pastor needs the Spirit's help is far from complete, but evidently his time was running out, and he wanted to remind his listeners (and later, his readers) that the Spirit's necessary assistance may be lost:

> [I]t is certain that ministers may lose the aid of the Holy Ghost. ... You shall not perish as believers, for everlasting life is in you; but you may perish as ministers, and be no more heard of as witnesses for the Lord.[39]

---

[35] *Lectures to My Students*, 196.
[36] *Lectures to My Students*, 196.
[37] *Lectures to My Students*, 197.
[38] *Lectures to My Students*, 197.
[39] *Lectures to My Students*, 199.

If this happens, there is surely a reason. Spurgeon gives a list of reasons, ranging from disobedience to the Spirit's promptings to neglect of private prayer. A gallery of individuals from Scripture who experienced the withdrawal of the Spirit's power then follows: some, like Balaam, were sons of perdition; others, like Samson, were children of God. In the light of these examples, Spurgeon can only pray for himself, his hearers and his readers: "O for the Spirit of God to make and keep us alive unto God, faithful to our office, and useful to our generation, and clear of the blood of men's souls."[40]

The Greatest Fight in the World

One of the main ways that Spurgeon kept in touch with graduates of the Pastors' College was through the College Conference. First held for five days in March of 1865, it was soon shifted to the month of September. An eagerly anticipated occasion, the annual conference helped to revive the flagging spirits of many of the graduates who labored in difficult circumstances in remote areas of the country or in urban areas hardened against the gospel and dangerous to health. The late 1880s, however, saw the disruption of this Conference as Spurgeon sought to repel what he rightly saw as the encroachment of liberal theology on English Baptist churches. A good number of the graduates of his College, though, failed to take his side in what came to be called the "Down-Grade controversy." The annual Conference was consequently re-formed and, from 1888 on, this re-formed Conference met in the month of April.[41]

---

[40] *Lectures to My Students*, 204.
[41] Nicholls, "Charles Haddon Spurgeon, Educationalist," 88–89.

The theme of the Conference in 1891, the last one that Spurgeon ever attended, was the work of the Spirit.[42] As the President of the Pastor's College, Spurgeon gave what was his customary Presidential address on the morning of Tuesday, April 21. This address, which took close to an hour and a half to deliver, was later published as *The Greatest Fight in the World* and was considered by Spurgeon as a concise declaration of his position vis-à-vis the Down-Grade controversy.

The address is divided into three parts: our armoury, namely, the Word of God; our army, namely, the church of God; and our strength, namely, the Spirit of God. Nearly half of the talk is devoted to a defence of God's Word as infallible and perfect, a reflection of the fact that among the central issues of the Down-Grade controversy was the nature of Scripture.

When Spurgeon comes to the final part of the address, he begins by highlighting the fact that the pastor's dependence upon the Spirit must be a practical reality, and not merely something theoretical. For instance, having read *The Gospel Worthy of All Acceptation* by the Calvinistic Baptist Andrew Fuller or *A Discourse Concerning the Holy Spirit* by the Puritan divine John Owen does not mean that one knows the truths which they discuss in these books. "We know nothing," Spurgeon maintains, "till we are taught by the Holy Ghost, who speaks to the heart."[43] Spurgeon then details a few areas in which the pastor must depend upon the Spirit, all of which would have been familiar territory to graduates of the Pastor's College who had heard Spurgeon's Friday afternoon lectures.

---

[42] For a report on this conference, see "Impressions of the Conference of 1891," *The Sword and the Trowel* (1891): 333–337.

[43] *The Greatest Fight in the World* (London: Passmore and Alabaster, 1891), 50.

From the work of the Spirit, Spurgeon turns to the pastor's experience of the Spirit and he gives his audience the timeless reminder that "when the Spirit of God is gone, even truth itself becomes an iceberg."[44] A few remarks on how best to secure the Spirit's help then follow. In this regard, Spurgeon especially urges his hearers never to consider the Holy Spirit as anything less than a fully divine person:

> Worship him [that is, the Spirit] as the adorable Lord God. Never call the Holy Spirit "it"; nor speak of him as if he were a doctrine, or an influence, or an orthodox myth. Reverence him, love him, and trust him with familiar yet reverent confidence. He is God, let him be God to you.[45]

Behind this statement is Spurgeon's concern that there was a slippage in English Baptist circles regarding the personhood of the Holy Spirit. Four years earlier, as noted above, Spurgeon had outlined a number of areas at the beginning of the Down-Grade controversy which he considered to be threatened by the inroads of liberal theology: "The Atonement is scouted, the inspiration of Scripture is derided, the Holy Spirit is degraded into an influence, the punishment of sin is turned into fiction, and the resurrection into a myth."[46]

While controversy over the personhood of the Spirit was not a prominent aspect of the Down-Grade controversy, Spurgeon was well aware that acceptance of the other key tenets of liberal theology invariably led to a rejection of this precious Biblical

---

[44] *Greatest Fight*, 56.

[45] *Greatest Fight*, 57.

[46] "Another Word concerning the Down-Grade," *The Sword and the Trowel* (1887): 397.

truth.[47] He would no doubt have appreciated the recent warning of Peter Berger, a Christian social scientist: "He who sups with the devil of modernity had better have a long spoon."[48] Firmly attached to the personhood of the Spirit from the earliest days of his ministry, Spurgeon was convinced that:

> A gospel without the Trinity!—it is a rope of sand that cannot hold together. ... Get the thought of the three persons, and you have the marrow of all divinity. Only know the Father, and know the Son, and know the Holy Ghost to be one, and all things will appear clear.[49]

In other words, the doctrine of three persons in one Godhead is an essential foundation to both the proclamation of the gospel and the study of theology.

Spurgeon concludes this address with a lengthy reminder of some things that the Spirit will never do. For instance, the Spirit will never bless compromises with doctrinal error or sin—a truth which had been burned afresh into Spurgeon's heart and soul during the Down-Grade controversy. Neither will the Spirit sanction laziness; he is no "friend of loiterers."[50] Nor will he have anything to do with those who preach not Christ.

> If we do not make the Lord Jesus glorious; if we do not lift him high in the esteem of men, if we do not labour to make him King of kings, and Lord of lords; we shall not have the Holy Spirit with us. Vain will be rhetoric, music,

---

[47] Cf. the remarks regarding the personhood of the Holy Spirit by [Robert Shindler], "Andover Theology," *The Sword and the Trowel* (1887): 274–280.

[48] Cited Os Guiness, "Let God Be God: Church Growth—Weaknesses to Watch," *Tabletalk* 16, No. 1 (February 1992): 53.

[49] "The Personality of the Holy Ghost," *The New Park Street Pulpit* (London: Passmore and Alabaster, 1856), 1:29.

[50] *Greatest Fight*, 59–62.

> architecture, energy, and social status: if our one design
> be not to magnify the Lord Jesus, we shall work alone and
> work in vain.[51]

Spurgeon made the same point somewhat more quaintly when he stated in his sermon "Receiving the Holy Ghost," preached in July of 1884: "the Holy Spirit always keeps sweet company with Jesus Christ."[52]

Many years before, when Spurgeon was in his first pastorate in the hamlet of Waterbeach, he had written a letter to his uncle in which he expressed the wish to be employed not only in Waterbeach but wherever he might be able to serve Christ. "I often wish," he wrote,

> I were in China, India, or Africa, so that I might preach, preach, preach all day long. It would be sweet to die preaching. But I want more of the Holy Spirit; I do not feel enough—no, not half enough,—of His Divine energy. "Come, Holy Spirit, come!" Then men must be converted; then the wicked would repent, and the just grow in grace.[53]

Quite evident in this letter, written when Spurgeon was but nineteen years of age, is Spurgeon's tremendous sensitivity to the absolute necessity of the help of the Holy Spirit in his preaching and ministry. It was a sensitivity that would stay with him throughout his life, as we have seen. It is a sensitivity that explains much about his remarkable ministry. Yet, it is also a sensitivity that serves as an encouragement and a challenge to us in our increasingly

---

[51] *Greatest Fight*, 64.

[52] *The Metropolitan Tabernacle Pulpit* (London: Passmore and Alabaster, 1885), 30:395.

[53] *The Letters of Charles Haddon Spurgeon*, collected and collated Charles Spurgeon, [Jr.] (Harrisburg: Good Books Corporation, [1923]), 54–55.

godless and needy age. Yes, indeed, "where the Spirit of God, there is power": power to live for Christ and power to bring glory to his person.

11

THE HOLY SPIRIT AND LOVE
OF THE BRETHREN

*The Spirit of God is given to the true saints to dwell in them,
as his proper lasting abode ... The light of the Sun of Righteousness
don't only shine upon them, but is so communicated to them,
that they shine also, and become little images of that Sun
which shines upon them...*

Jonathan Edwards
(1703–1758)

Historically my Baptist forebears have had a great interest in answering questions about the church, questions like: Who belongs to the church? Who has authority in the church? Is there such a thing as the universal church? Among the most important of these questions is one that received a lot of attention in the early years when Baptists emerged from the matrix of Puritanism, namely, what are the marks of a true church? In other words, what distinguishes a true church from a false church? Seventeenth-century Baptists argued that a true church was one in which the Word of God was preached, the ordinances of baptism and the Lord's Supper properly administered and biblical discipline carried out. At the close of the eighteenth century, Baptists began to argue that mission was also vital to the identity of a true church. "The true churches of Jesus Christ," Andrew Fuller wrote in 1810, "travail in birth for the salvation of men. They are the armies of the Lamb, the grand object of whose existence is to extend the Redeemer's kingdom."[1] Now, without taking away one particle from either of these historic Baptist perspectives, a close reading of the New Testament compels us to further affirm that a true church is marked out as a community of Christ-like love. Love is an indelible mark of a New Testament church. And this is because New Testament congregations were places where the Spirit was present in power, and chief among his works and fruit is love.

When the Apostle Paul came to list the effects of the Spirit's work within Christians, for instance, the first that he took note of was "love."[2] It is also the Spirit who makes the love of God for us a reality,[3] and who enables believers to love one another.[4] But love is not only a gift of the Spirit, but is also very much a human response and act. Thus, Paul tells the Ephesians, for example, to "walk in love, as Christ loved us and gave himself up for us."[5] He reminds Timothy, and the Ephesian church through this dear brother, that the goal of Christian preaching and teaching is "love that issues from a pure heart and a good conscience and a sincere faith."[6] The writer of Hebrews is content with a more simple admonition, "Let brotherly love continue"[7] as is Peter when the latter urges the believers in Asia Minor to "love the brethren."[8] It is especially in the writings of the Apostle John, however, that love

---

[1] *The Promise of the Spirit, the Grand Encouragement in Promoting the Gospel Friend* in *The Complete Works of the Rev. Andrew Fuller*, revised Joseph Belcher (3rd London ed.; repr. Harrisonburg: Sprinkle Publications, 1988), III, 359.

[2] Galatians 5:22.

[3] Romans 5:5.

[4] Colossians 1:8.

[5] Ephesians 5:2 ESV.

[6] 1 Timothy 1:5 ESV.

[7] Hebrews 13:1.

[8] 1 Peter 2:17.

of the brethren in particular and the language of love in general is to be found.[9]

1 John: its context and teaching on love

Consider one of these texts, 1 John, written by the Apostle John towards the end of a long life when he was most probably living in the great urban center of Ephesus.[10] In part, the letter is a Spirit-breathed response to a dire heresy that was threatening the spirituality and unity of the church in that city and the surrounding region. The heretics concerned denied the reality of the Incarnation[11] and also appear to have been scornful of living lives of holiness.[12] Although these heretics had left the Ephesian church,[13] John was still profoundly concerned for the health of this community of believers. Among the things John thus stresses so as to secure the unity of this Christian body is that genuine followers of Jesus Christ not only love God but they love all in whom God dwells. In John's words: "everyone who loves the Father loves whoever has been born of him"[14] and the proof that "we have passed out of death into life" is that "we love the brothers."[15]

"What great love"

Now, the Apostle stresses three things in particular about this love of the brethren. First, it is a direct result of being overwhelmed with the love of God. John is utterly amazed at the magnificence

---

[9] Robert W. Yarbrough, *1–3 John* (Baker Exegetical Commentary on the New Testament; Grand Rapids: Baker Publishing Group, 2008), 174–175; *idem*, "Introduction to 1 John," *ESV Study Bible* (Wheaton: Crossway Bibles, 2008), 2425.

[10] See Georg Strecker, *The Johannine Letters*, trans. Linda M. Maloney and ed. Harold Attridge (Hermeneia: Fortress Press, 1996), xl–xli for Ephesus as the place of composition.

[11] 1 John 4:1–6. See also 2 John 7.

[12] 1 John 3:4–10.

[13] 1 John 2:19.

[14] 1 John 5:1 ESV.

[15] 1 John 3:14 ESV.

of the love of God for sinners. "Look at what great love the Father has given to us," he urges his readers.[16] We should never think that we, out of hearts naturally filled with affection, decided to lovingly embrace God prior to his coming into our lives. We were in a state of death[17]: utterly unresponsive to divine love and totally unconcerned about divine purposes. "We love," John insists, "because he first loved us."[18]

One theologian who sought to emphasize this truth throughout his ministry was the North African Augustine of Hippo, who, in his eloquent account of how the God of love and love of God pursued him over the course of years, makes the same point as John thus:

> I have learnt to love you late, Beauty at once so ancient and so new! I have learnt to love you late! ... You called me; you cried aloud to me; you broke my barrier of deafness. You shone upon me; your radiance enveloped me; you put my blindness to my flight. You shed your fragrance about me; I drew breath and now I gasp for your sweet odour. I tasted you, and now I hunger and thirst for you. You touched me, and I am inflamed with love of your peace.[19]

"O the sweet exchange"

Second, this love of God to which we respond is a love supremely shown in the death of Christ in the place of sinners: "this is love, not that we have loved God but that he loved us and sent his Son to be the propitiation for our sins."[20] John's point here is well seen

---

16 1 John 3:1 Author's translation. See also Yarbrough, *1–3 John*, 175.

17 1 John 3:14.

18 1 John 4:19.

19 *Confessions* 10.27, trans. R.S. Pine-Coffin (London: Penguin Books, 1961), 231–232.

20 1 John 4:10.

in another patristic text, this time one written towards the end of the second century, when a pagan by the name of Diognetus was struck by the fact that early Christian communities were communities of love, something quite different from his pagan experience of social relationships. He asked a Christian he knew, a man who had a rich command of written Greek, what it was that made Christians love each other so much.[21] This author, whose name has not come down to us, took Diognetus to the cross and there showed him the deep love of Christ for sinners. "O the exceeding kindness and love of God," this Christian author was constrained to cry out. Despite the fact that we had committed sins worthy of punishment and death and the fact that we were "wicked and impious," God "did not hate or reject us."[22] Rather,

> in mercy he took our sins upon himself. He himself gave his own Son as a ransom for us—the Holy One for the godless, the Innocent One for the wicked, the Righteous One for the unrighteous, the Incorruptible for the corruptible, the Immortal for the mortal. For what else was able to cover our sins except his righteousness? In whom could we, who were lawless and godless, have been justified, but in the Son of God alone? O the sweet exchange! O the inscrutable work of God! O blessings beyond all expectation!—that the wickedness of many should be hidden in the one Righteous Man, and the righteousness of the One should justify the many wicked![23]

Little wonder this Christian exclaims "O the sweet exchange" in the middle of this tremendous passage. To think

---

[21] *Letter to Diognetus* 1.
[22] *Letter to Diognetus* 9.1–2, 4.
[23] *Letter to Diognetus* 9.2–5.

that my sins—all of them, no exceptions—my sins of commission—thinking things I ought not to have thought, saying things I ought not to have said, doing things I ought not to have done—and my sins of omission—not thinking things I ought to have thought, not saying things I ought to have said, not doing things I ought to have done—sins that deserve the full fury of hell, have been laid on the dear head of the Son—the Lord Jesus—and he has borne them all. Is this not what John means when he says that God "loved us and sent his Son to be the propitiation for our sins"? But there is more, as the letter to Diognetus makes clear. As a result of the love embedded in the cross-work of Christ, I, who once deserved hell, have been clothed in Christ's lived-out holiness— "O the sweet exchange!"

Now, the Christian author asks his pagan friend, once "you have acquired this knowledge [of God's love], with what joy do you suppose you will be filled? Or how will you love him who so first loved you?"[24] Christians love one another because God first loved them and showed that love through the sacrificial gift of his own beloved Son for them.

"We ought to lay down our lives for the brothers"

Third, having experienced this wondrous love of God, we ought to love others as God in Christ has loved us: "by this we know love, that he laid down his life for us, and we ought to lay down our lives for the brothers."[25] Our love for one another is to be an imitation of the love of Christ for us.

How weird this must have sounded in the ears of many of John's pagan contemporaries. The Stoic philosopher Seneca (4BC-65AD), for instance, in his book *On tranquillity of mind* (*c.*50), notes

---

[24] *Letter to Diognetus* 10.3.
[25] 1 John 3:16 ESV.

how easy it is to be seized by "hatred of the human race" and overwhelmed with misery when we see all of the corruption and vice around us in society. What strategy did he propose to dispel such hatred? Well, he suggested:

> All things must be made light of and borne with a calm mind: it is more manlike to scoff at life than to bewail it. Furthermore, he who laughs at the human race also deserves better of it than he who mourns for it. The former leaves something still to be hoped for; the latter stupidly weeps over what he despairs of being able to correct: and he shows a greater mind who, after he has contemplated all things, cannot restrain his laughter than he who cannot restrain his tears, inasmuch as he does not allow his mind to be affected in the least, and does not consider anything great, severe, or even serious.[26]

For Seneca, then, the cure for hatred is "flippant ridicule" and sheer cynicism.[27] And how often have we, God's people, gone down this path when it comes to dealing with brothers and sisters with whom we disagree. Rather than express hatred for them, we mock them behind their backs, ridicule them for their beliefs, make fun of them and write them off. But John knows a better way: love like that of Christ that is forgetful of self and concerned primarily for the other.

Of course, there is a fundamental difference between Christ's laying down his life for us and what we do for others. His was an atonement for our sins. At most, our following Christ in

---

[26] *On tranquility of mind* 15.1–3, trans. William Bell Langsdorf (New York: G.P. Putnam's Sons, 1900), revised and ed. Michael S. Russo (2000; http://www.molloy.edu/sophia/seneca/tranquility.htm; accessed October 29, 2008). I am indebted to Yarbrough, *1–3 John*, 202, for alerting me to this text by Seneca.

[27] Yarbrough, *1–3 John*, 202.

this path of self-denying love will result in martyrdom.[28] In fact, lest John's readers think that martyrdom is what he primarily has in mind, he immediately adds: "If anyone has the world's goods and sees his brother in need, yet closes his heart against him, how does God's love abide in him?"[29] There might well be an occasion when imitation of Christ's love demands martyrdom, but surely most frequently this imitation will take place in the hurly-burly of everyday life.[30]

I shall never forget an important lesson I learned in this regard in my first year of seminary. There were a dozen of us that year who started the master's program at Wycliffe College in the University of Toronto, then a small evangelical Anglican (Episcopalian) seminary. It was clear that of the twelve, eleven or so were solidly evangelical, but some of us had our doubts about one of our fellow students. We thought he was kind of "high Church," which in Anglican jargon meant that he was closer to Roman Catholicism than evangelicalism. We used to joke about his having a statue of Mary in his closet and make other snide remarks about him behind his back.

Well, it was one late October day of our second year of studies. This brother came to me with a book he had purchased at an annual book sale held in the final week of October by one of the other colleges at the University, Trinity College, which was right across the road from Wycliffe College where I was studying. It still happens and it is a tremendous book sale for anyone with an interest in biblical studies, theology, or church history for they always have tons of books in those areas. Well, this student had

---

[28] Daniel Akin, *1, 2, 3 John* (New American Commentary, v.38; Nashville: Broadman and Holman, 2001), 158.

[29] 1 John 3:17 ESV.

[30] I. Howard Marshall, *The Epistles of John* (Grand Rapids: Wm. B. Eerdmans, 1978), 194–196.

come across a paperback version of the Greek edition of Athanasius' *On the incarnation of the Word*. He knew that I was deeply interested in the Fathers and he bought it specially for me. I was humbled by his love. I had treated him as Seneca recommended, with scorn and disdain. But he had loved me as a brother in Christ and as Christ had loved the Church.

Love and the Spirit

Finally, when we love one another in the way described above, we can be sure that God indwells us: "if we love one another," John notes, "God abides in us."[31] And the means of this indwelling is none other than the blessed person of the Holy Spirit. On two distinct occasions John affirms this as something all genuine Christians know: "we know that he abides in us"—how?—"by the Spirit whom he has given us."[32] Love for the brethren thus serves to confirm the reality of our faith.

Moreover, why are Christians capable of loving one another as described by 1 John? For the basic reason that they are indwelt by the Spirit of God. His coming into the lives of men and women launches a revolution—a revolution of love!

Some implications

Let me draw out two implications that flow out of John's admonition to love our brothers and sisters along the lines of the template of Christ's love. First of all, it is obvious that if you are going to love the brethren you must belong to a body of believers, for that is the place where you discover the needs of other Christians and can extend to them Christ-like love. In fact, one early Southern Baptist, Oliver Hart (1723–1795), pastor of First

---

[31] 1 John 4:12.
[32] 1 John 3:24. See also 1 John 4:13.

Baptist Church in Charleston, South Carolina, from 1750 to 1780, saw in the biblical admonition to love the brethren an argument for the necessity of Baptist associations. As he stated in 1791:

> Although churches are independent of each other, with respect to power and government, yet the gospel they profess binds them to hold communion, in brotherly love [and] fellowship … Brotherly love is essential to Christianity, and necessarily exists, not only between believers, as individuals, but between gospel churches; especially those of the same faith and order. These ought to hold fellowship with each other.[33]

Then, we have to realize that it is in the love shown to the brethren that the reality of our faith is revealed. In the words of the Puritan divine John Owen: "the apostle John … wrote his First Epistle almost to this very end and purpose—to let us know, that there was neither … evidence of the love of God to us, nor of our love to God, unless there was fervent and intense love towards the brethren."[34] As you read the history of the church it is not uncommon to come across an individual seemingly passionate in his love for Christ, but whose treatment of brothers and sisters with whom he disagreed has made the gospel of Christ's love seem a sham.

A concluding example

In the late 160s the Syrian humorist Lucian of Samosata (*c.*120–*c.*180), subsequently recognized as one of the most important literary figures of his day, wrote a biting satire about a Cynic

---

[33] *A Gospel Church portrayed and her Costly Service pointed out* (Trenton, 1791), 31.
[34] *Gospel Charity* in *The Works of John Owen*, ed. William H. Goold (1850–1853 ed.; repr. Edinburgh/Carlisle: The Banner of Truth Trust, 1965), IX, 259.

philosopher by the name of Peregrinus, who had ended his days by burning himself to death on a pyre at the Olympic Games in 165.[35] For a while, Peregrinus, whom Lucian regarded as a rank charlatan, had adopted Christianity and according to Lucian, was even imprisoned for his Christian profession. Lucian described the way other Christians responded to Peregrinus' imprisonment:

> When Peregrinus was put in prison, the Christians thought it a terrible disaster, and did everything they could to try and get him out. When this proved impossible, they helped him in every other way they could think of. First thing every morning, you would see a crowd of old women, widows, and orphans waiting outside the prison ... They brought him in all sorts of food, talked to him about their religion, and called "that good man Peregrinus" (for that was how they spoke of him) a second Socrates. Delegates even arrived from other Christian communities in Asia Minor, to help him by petitioning for his release and trying to comfort him.

Lucian then went on to comment about the gullibility of Christians in general—a comment that speaks powerfully of the nature of early Christian communities in the Roman Imperium.

> They are always incredibly quick off the mark, when one of them gets into trouble like this—in fact they ignore their own interests completely. Why, they actually sent him large sums of money by way of compensation for his imprisonment, so that he made a considerable profit out of them! For the poor souls have persuaded themselves that they are immortal and will live for ever. As a result, they

---

[35] For the dating, see A.M. Harmon, "Lucian of Samosata: The Passing of Peregrinus," n.22 (http://www.tertullian.org/rpearse/lucian/peregrinus.htm; accessed October 24, 2008).

think nothing of death, and most of them are perfectly willing to sacrifice themselves. Besides, their first law-giver [that is, Christ] has convinced them that once they stop believing in Greek gods, and start worshipping that crucified sage of theirs, and living according to his laws, they are all each other's brothers and sisters. So, taking this information on trust, without any guarantee of its truth, they think nothing else matters, and believe in common ownership—which means that any unscrupulous adventurer who comes along can soon make a fortune out of them, for the silly creatures are very easily taken in.[36]

On the basis of their devotion to Christ, their deeply-held conviction that eternal realities are more important than merely temporal matters, and their fundamental belief that those who are in Christ are brothers and sisters, these early Christians were able to show true generosity and genuine love to one another. Lucian viewed their love for one another with derision. Later commentators, like the twentieth-century patristic scholar Henry Chadwick, have seen in this love of believers "probably the most potent single cause" of the growth of the church during the early Roman Imperium.[37] In other words, the Spirit grew the Church in those early centuries, and he did so chiefly through love.

---

[36] *The Passing of Peregrinus* 11–13 (trans. Paul Turner, *Lucian: Satirical Sketches* [Harmondsworth: Penguin Books Ltd., 1961], 11).

[37] Henry Chadwick, *The Early Church* (Rev. ed.; London: Penguin Books, 1993), 56.

12

Rediscovering the Sacred:
Testing the spirits of postmodernity[1]

*He who has an ear, let him hear
what the Spirit says to the churches.*

Revelation 2:7, 11, 17, 29; 3:6, 13, 22 ESV.

"Better free your mind instead"

It was in the spring of 1968 after John Lennon (1940–1980) and his fellow Beatles had spent some time in a Himalayan retreat with the Maharishi Mahesh Yogi (1917–2008) that Lennon began to write a song that presciently summarized the massive change that would take place in the worldview of the West over the next few decades. That year there was a brutal shift from the emphasis on love and peace that had characterized the counter-culture to violence and revolution. Violent confrontations between state authorities and students throughout major European and American cities were a familiar phenomenon throughout the year and the talk of revolution was in the air.[2] Lennon, though, refused to let go of the hippie ideals of love and peace. The song would be simply entitled *Revolution 1*:

---

[1] This chapter had its origins as a paper that was delivered at the Annual Meeting of the American Association of Christian Colleges and Seminaries, Inc., February 4, 2009.

[2] For the historical context of *Revolution 1*, see Ian Macdonald, *Revolution in the Head: The Beatles' Records and the Sixties* (London: Pimlico, 1995), 223–229; Philip Norman, *John Lennon: The Life* (Doubleday, 2008), 553–555.

167

You say you want a revolution,
well, you know,
we all want to change the world.
You tell me that it's evolution,
well, you know
we all want to change the world.
But when you talk about destruction,
Don't you know you can count me out. …
You say you'll change the constitution,
well, you know,
we all want to change your head.
You tell me it's the institution,
well, you know,
you better free your mind instead.
But if you go carrying pictures of Chairman Mao,
You ain't going to make it with anyone anyhow.[3]

Though condemned as a betrayal of the counter-culture by the New Left at the time, this song well captures the essence of what has taken place in western society during these past four decades. The political revolution that the New Left had sought in the 1960s had fizzled out by the middle of the next decade. Nevertheless, there has been a massive revolution, but it has been a "revolution in the head" in which men and women have sought, consciously or unconsciously, to heed Lennon's advice and "free [their minds] instead." Pundits have labeled this revolution in mindset as "postmodernism" in contrast to "modernity" that was the hegemonic worldview from the eighteenth-century Enlightenment to the 1960s.

---

[3] *The Beatles Lyrics* (London: Warner Books, 1995), 152.

Rediscovering the sacred

Modernity exulted in the omnicompetence of human reason to discover universal truths through science, naïvely asserted the inevitability of material and technological progress, and assiduously cultivated a total indifference to religion.[4] Postmodernism, in contrast, prizes relativism, rejects the possibility of framing a coherent metanarrative for all of life, has serious questions about the unqualified beneficence of technology, and is fascinated with "spirituality" to the point that the latter has become "a growth industry" in contemporary western culture.[5] Various plausible explanations have been given for the rediscovery of the sacred in postmodern culture, ranging from the counter-culture's heavy use in the Sixties of the drug d-lysergic acid diethylamide (LSD or acid) to transcend the "straitjacket" of the rational self[6] to the

---

[4] A telling example of modernity's indifference to religion can be found in a comment made by Paul Tillich in 1963 to the effect that the adjective "spiritual" had so faded from usage in western culture—it was "lost beyond hope"—that he was not going to use it in his discussion of the Christian life. See his *Systematic Theology* (Chicago: University of Chicago Press, 1963), III, 22. I owe this reference to Martin E. Marty, "Materialism and Spirituality in American Religion" in Robert Wuthnow, ed., *Rethinking Materialism: Perspectives on the Spiritual Dimension of Economic Behavior* (Grand Rapids: Wm. B. Eerdmans, 1995), 252.

[5] On postmodernism and its contrast with modernity, see especially Stanley J. Grenz, *A Primer on Postmodernism* (Grand Rapids/Cambridge: Wm. B. Eerdmans, 1996), for an engaging overview. See also the various essays in the following works: David S. Dockery, ed., *the Challenge of Postmodernism: An Evangelical Engagement* (Grand Rapids: Baker Books, 1995); D.A. Carson, ed., *Telling the Truth: Evangelizing Postmoderns* (Grand Rapids: Zondervan, 2000); Steven Connor, ed., *The Cambridge Companion to Postmodernism* (Cambridge: Cambridge University Press, 2004). The remarks about spirituality are from Richard Lovelace, *Renewal as a Way of Life* (Downers Grove: InterVarsity Press, 1985), 15.

[6] See, for example, John Allan, *Shopping for God: Fringe religions today* (Grand Rapids: Baker Book House, 1986), 62–67; Phyllis Tickle, *The Great Emergence: How Christianity Is Changing and Why* (Grand Rapids: Baker Books, 2008), 97–98. At the height of the counter-culture in the Sixties, LSD was being taken by several million people.

It is noteworthy that Eckhart Tolle, who has become a central figure in the booming interest in spirituality (see below), also points to the "hippie movement" as making it "possible for ancient Eastern wisdom and spirituality to move west and play an essential part" in what Tolle calls "the awakening of global consciousness" (Eckhart Tolle, *A New Earth: Awakening to Your Life's True Purpose* [London: Plume, 2005], 92–93).

pervasive influence of the thinking of the German philosopher Martin Heidegger (1889–1976), who in his later work lambasted modernity's indifference to the sacred and asserted "only a god can save us."[7]

From a Christian standpoint, the torrential interest in the sacred and spirituality that has flooded contemporary culture is also readily understandable from the fact that to be human is to be *homo adorans*. Men and women were made to worship the living God. And if they will not worship him, they will worship gods of their own making. As the French Reformer John Calvin once rightly remarked, the human heart is "a perpetual factory of idols."[8] Calvin argued that within the structure of every human existence there is an instinctual awareness of God. Human beings know God with the immediacy that they know the surrounding cosmos and even themselves.[9] Calvin used various terms to designate this innate knowledge—"an awareness of divinity" (*divinitatis sensus*),[10] for example, and "seed of religion" (*semen religionis*)[11]—but it has been so damaged by the Fall that it cannot issue in anything but idolatry, and "so it happens that no real piety remains in the world."[12] The critical term in this quote is the

---

[7] Cited S.J. McGrath, *Heidegger: A (Very) Critical Introduction* (Grand Rapids/Cambridge: Wm. B. Eerdmans, 2008), 120. McGrath's study is an excellent analysis of Heideggerian thought from a Christian perspective. For the influence of Heidegger on postmodern thinking, also see Philippa Berry, "Postmodernism and post-religion" in Connor, ed., *Cambridge Companion to Postmodernism*, 174.

[8] *Institutes* 1.11.8 (*Calvin: Institutes of the Christian Religion*, trans. Ford Lewis Battles and ed. John T. McNeill [The Library of Christian Classics, vol. 20; Philadelphia: The Westminster Press, 1960], 108). Subsequent references to the *Institutes* will employ this edition, but will simply identify the reference or quote by book, chapter, and section with the page number in brackets.

[9] John H. Leith, *From Generation to Generation: The Renewal of the Church According to its own Theology and Practice* (Louisville: Westminster John Knox Press, 1990), 46.

[10] *Institutes* 1.3.1: "There is within the human mind, and indeed by natural instinct, an awareness of divinity," 43.

[11] *Institutes* 1.4.1: "As experience shows, God has sown a seed of religion in all men," 47.

[12] *Institutes* 1.4.1, 47.

adjective "real." Given his understanding of the fundamental religiosity of all of humanity, the "rediscovery of the sacred" by postmodern Western culture would not have surprised him in the least.[13]

Nomenclature

The etymological origin of the English term "spirituality" can be traced back to the Latin term *spiritualitas* which, in turn, is derived from the noun *spiritus* ("spirit") and the adjectives *spiritalis* or *spiritualis* ("spiritual"). In Christian speech the latter are translations of the Greek *pneuma* and *pneumatikos*, which, in the New Testament, are regularly used of the Holy Spirit and that which lies under his control.[14] *Spiritualitas* first appears in a letter that has traditionally been ascribed to Jerome (*c*.347–420), the key translator behind the Latin Vulgate, although recently the text has been variously attributed to Faustus of Riez (died *c*.490), Pelagius (*fl*.400–410) or an anonymous author from within the Pelagian circle. The author's correspondent is urged to "act so as to grow in spirituality."[15] While the word was not commonly used over the

---

[13] For accounts of this rediscovery, see, for example, Wade Clark Roof, *A Generation of Seekers: The Spiritual Journeys of the Baby Boom Generation* (New York: HarperCollins, 1993); *idem, Spiritual Marketplace: Baby Boomers and the Remaking of American Religion* (Princeton: Princeton University Press, 1999); Robert Wuthnow, *After Heaven: Spirituality in America since the 1950s* (Berkeley/Los Angeles: University of California Press, 1998).

[14] Declan Marmion, *A Spirituality of Everyday Faith: A Theological Investigation of the Notion of Spirituality in Karl Rahner* (Louvain: Peeters Press, 1998), 4.

[15] Cited Walter Principe, "Towards defining spirituality," *Studies in Religion* 12, no.2 (Spring 1983): 130–131. See also Marmion, *Spirituality of Everyday Faith* 10 and n.26–27; Paul Rorem, "Augustine For and Against "Spirituality," *inSpire* 6, no.2 (Winter 2002): 12–13; *idem*, "Augustine for and against contemporary 'spirituality'" in *Currents in Theology and Mission* (April 2003) (http://findarticles.com/p/articles/mi_m0MDO/is_2_30/ai_99699733; accessed January 28, 2009).

According to T.R. Albin, the term *spiritualitas* owes its origin to French Catholicism—he does not mention the French word, but presumably he is thinking of the word *spiritualité*—and it did not emerge as a "well-defined branch of theology until the 18th century" ("Spirituality" in Sinclair B. Ferguson and David F. Wright, *New Dictionary of Theology* [Downers Grove/Leicester: InterVarsity Press, 1988], 656).

next seven centuries, the word denoted roughly what today we would describe as the Christian life. In this early use of the term, as opposed to later developments in the High Middle Ages where it came to be a synonym for incorporeality and a term designating the clergy,[16] the New Testament idea of life according to the Holy Spirit predominates. Given the development of the word during the Middle Ages, though, it is not surprising that central figures in the Reformation, like Calvin, preferred to use another Latin term, namely, *pietas*, to designate a life devoted to God through the power of the Spirit of Christ.[17]

Nevertheless, given its roots in the Latin term for Spirit, the word "spirituality" can helpfully remind us that biblical spirituality is intimately bound up with the Holy Spirit and his work. Essentially, biblical spirituality is a spirituality of response to the presence and work of the Holy Spirit, a spirituality that is ultimately his creation.[18] In the first place, it is he who enables sinners estranged from God in mind, will and affections to respond to God's graciousness in the person and work of Jesus Christ. According to Paul, for example, it is the Holy Spirit who makes God's grace and love real for men and women—"God's love has been poured into our hearts through the Holy Spirit."[19] It is through his power alone that a person can then embrace Jesus Christ as Savior and Lord—"no one can say, 'Jesus is Lord' except in the Holy Spirit."[20] And from then on, it is the Spirit who

---

[16] Marmion, *Spirituality of Everyday Faith*, 12–14.

[17] Ralph C. Wood, "Outward Faith, Inward Piety: The Dependence of Spirituality on Worship and Doctrine" in Timothy George and Alister McGrath, eds., *For All the Saints: Evangelical Theology and Christian Spirituality* (Louisville: Westminster John Knox Press, 2003), 94–96.

[18] See the logic in Ephesians 2:1–10, for example. God saves helpless sinners without any consideration of their works that their lives might henceforth be filled with "good works."

[19] Romans 5:5.

[20] 1 Corinthians 12:3.

undergirds and empowers the entirety of believers' lives in Christ. For this very reason the apostle argues that "if we live by the Spirit"—if we have been given spiritual life by the Spirit—"let us also walk by the Spirit"—let us live lives marked by genuine dependence on and submission to the Spirit of God.[21]

The problem with the term "spirituality," though, is the staggering breadth of its current usage. Being spiritual and spirituality are in vogue. In the words of Charles Nienkirchen: "A spiritual hunger gnaws at the soul of the post-modern culture which is readily exploited by an array of special interest groups ..."[22] In an article in *Newsweek* from 2005 it was noted that 79% of people in a poll around that time described themselves as "spiritual." "Everywhere we looked," Jerry Adler, the lead writer of the article, noted, there is "a flowering of spirituality," though this has not resulted in "an explosion of people going to church."[23] This flowering is seen in bulletin boards in public libraries advertising meditation, journaling and dream interpretation classes, in demonstrations of yoga and Tai Chi in shopping malls and bookstores like Barnes & Noble, in the burgeoning New Age section of those same bookstores, in the fascination of television talk show hosts and our media with the supernatural and the occult, in the use of mediums to help in police investigations. In a popular piece on this resurgence of interest in so-called spirituality, Edith M. Humphrey, a Canadian scholar, noted that a random search of the web based on the term "spirituality" turned up the following web-sites:

Spirituality for Today; Women's Spirituality Book List; The Spirited Walker: Fitness Walking for Clarity,

---

[21] Galatians 5:25.

[22] "Going 'spiritual' in the 1990s," *Christian Week* (February 15, 1994): 8.

[23] "In Search of Spirituality," *Newsweek* (August 29/September 5, 2005): 49.

> Balance, and Spiritual Connection; ... Jesuit Spirituality;
> Native American Spirituality; ... Spirit Tools for a New
> Age (pyramids, wands, daggers, and pendulums ...);
> Spirituality and Health; Spirituality and Living Longer;
> The Inner Self Magazine: Spirituality as Opposed to Re-
> ligion; Spirituality in the Workplace; Sex and Spiritual-
> ity: Frequently Asked Questions; Apply Spiritual Ideas
> in Practical Ways; Spirituality Book—the invisible Path
> to Success; Psychotherapy and Spirituality; The Spir-
> itual Walk of the Labyrinth.[24]

Looking at this mishmash, it is not surprising that some Christians are extremely hesitant to use the term "spirituality." The word seems to mean everything and consequently nothing! What soon becomes clear, though, in any investigation of this contemporary obsession with spirituality is that while much of it is superficial, vacuous, and commodified—even tailor-made to fit individual desires and beliefs—it is feeding off of a deep hunger in millions of people in the West.[25]

The postmodern spirituality of Eckhart Tolle

A good example of contemporary spirituality is that promoted by Eckhart Tolle (1948–), whose books have become bestsellers, largely through the influence of media mogul Oprah Winfrey (1954–), his most famous disciple, and who has been touted by

---

[24] "It's Not About Us: Generic Spirituality and the Christian," *Christianity Today* 45, no.5 (April 2, 2001): 68. For two overviews of the variety of spiritualities that have emerged since the 1970s, see, from quite different perspectives, Peter Jones, *Spirit Wars: Pagan Revival in Christian America* (Mukilteo: WinePress Publishing/Escondido: Main Entry Editions, 1997), 209–233 and William Martin, "Embracing the Lite" in Arvind Sharma, ed., *Religion in a Secular City: Essays in Honor of Harvey Cox* (Harrisburg: Trinity Press International, 2001), 249–262.

[25] Marty, "Materialism and Spirituality," 252–253; Martin, "Embracing the Lite," 259.

Science of Mind magazine as their "spiritual hero of the year."[26] When he was twenty-nine, after living through a period of severe anxiety, interspersed with suicidal depression, Tolle experienced a life-changing transformation in which he realized that his "self," which was based on his limited, thinking mind, was not his true identity at all. His true identity, and that of everyone, is "the One Life, the One Consciousness that is prior to egoic identity."[27] According to one account, following this experience of "enlightenment," Tolle, who was living in England at the time,

> lost all interest in worldly activities, He dropped out of school, quit his job as a teaching assistant, and sat on a park bench for two years. Many assumed he was homeless. Others began to come to him with questions. Thus began his life as a spiritual teacher.[28]

Generalizing from his own experience, Tolle teaches that everything by which we form an understanding of who we are—rational thinking, emotional and affective responses, the capacity to will and remember—is actually an illusion. Rather, the "ultimate truth of who you are is not I am this or I am that, but I Am."[29] Tolle is undoubtedly aware that this term "I Am" is used in Scripture as a divine name.[30] In other words, he is affirming that a

---

[26] Warren G. Nozaki, "Paradise Still Lost in Eckhart Tolle's *A New Earth*," *Christian Research Journal* 31, no.5 (2008): 12; Front cover of *Science of Mind* 82, no.1 (January 2009).

[27] Tolle, *A New Earth*, 27–34; Donna Mosher, "The Power in the Present Moment," *Science of Mind* 82, no.1 (January 2009): 10; Nozaki, "Paradise Still Lost," 12.

[28] Mosher, "Power in the Present Moment," 10.

[29] Tolle, *A New Earth*, 57.

[30] See, for example, Exodus 3:14. Out of thirty-one endnotes in Tolle, *A New Earth*, 311–313, for example, twenty refer to Scripture texts. Nearly always Tolle reads into these texts his own personal philosophy. On Tolle's misuse of Scripture, see Nozaki, "Paradise Still Lost," 17. He can even misapply a quotation from Augustine in support of his views. See Tolle, *A New Earth*, 72. Beyond these actual quotations of Scripture texts, Tolle frequently refers to Jesus in his books. See, for example, *A New Earth*, 104, 220, 254.

person's real identity is to be found in the fact that he or she is ontologically one with what Tolle variously calls "the Truth," "Consciousness," or "Being."[31] There is little doubt that Tolle is promoting a form of monistic pantheism, even though he rarely uses the term "God."[32] And in typical postmodern fashion, Tolle disparages rational thought, stating bluntly that it is "the root of the ego" and "the wisdom of this world" condemned by Paul in 1 Corinthians 3:19.[33] Finally, Tolle makes a sharp distinction between spirituality, on the one hand, and religion, on the other. The latter is based on dogma and a rigid "belief system—a set of thoughts that you regard as the absolute truth," whereas the former has to do with "the transformation of consciousness."[34] But this distinction is also quintessentially postmodern, although recent research indicates that a majority of North American adults refuse to see religion and spirituality as mutually exclusive.[35]

Listening to the Spirit and developing true spirituality

While it is relatively easy to critique such eclectic, postmodern spirituality from a biblical standpoint,[36] the development of a truly biblical spirituality has not proven as easy for Evangelicals in the past thirty years or so. One approach that has proven quite popular makes significant use of Roman Catholic literature, based on

---

[31] Tolle, *A New Earth*, 71.

[32] Tolle claims that the word "God" has been so misused for thousands of years that it has been emptied of all meaning. See *A New Earth*, 220; Nozaki, "Paradise Still Lost," 14. For rare uses of the term "God," see *A New Earth*, 106, 251, 261, 267.

[33] *A New Earth*, 55, 196.

[34] *A New Earth*, 17–18. It is interesting that President Obama, at a National Prayer Breakfast in early 2009, stated that his "mother ... was skeptical of organized religion, even as she was the kindest, most spiritual person I've ever known" "Remarks of President Barack Obama National Prayer Breakfast" (http://i.usatoday.net/news/TheOval/Obama-prayer-breakfast-2-5-2009.pdf; accessed February 8, 2009).

[35] Rodney Stark, *What Americans Really Believe: New Findings from the Baylor Surveys of Religion* (Waco: Baylor University Press, 2008), 87–94.

[36] See, for example, Nozaki, "Paradise Still Lost," 10–19.

the false assumption that Evangelicals have a great expertise with regard to matters relating to conversion but are mere novices when it comes to the charting of the Christian life.[37] But there is a wealth of literature from the Puritan era and that of classical, eighteenth-century Evangelicalism that is deeply rooted in Scripture and that deals with all areas of the Christian life from regeneration to glorification. One paradigmatic study of this literature that I have found particularly helpful is Richard F. Lovelace's *Dynamics of Spiritual Life* and his *Renewal as a Way of Life*, the latter designed for a more popular audience.[38]

Lovelace, currently emeritus professor of church history at Gordon-Conwell Theological Seminary in Wenham, Massachusetts, helpfully begins his reflection on spiritual renewal and the Christian life by looking at its theological foundations in what he calls "preconditions of renewal" and "primary elements of renewal."[39] The former comprise a profound awareness of the majestic holiness of God and a corresponding understanding of the depth of sin in the human heart. The latter are the basic theological perspectives that must undergird any spirituality that is truly biblical: justification by faith alone and its fruit, a robust sanctification, the reality of the indwelling Holy Spirit and the nature of spiritual warfare against the world, the flesh and the devil. Once these preconditions and primary elements of spirituality are in place, then one can focus on such spiritual disciplines as mission,

---

[37] See, for example, Brian McLaren, *Finding Our Way Again: The Return of the Ancient Practices* (Nashville: Thomas Nelson, 2008). See also this author's critique of this book: "Recovering Ancient Church Practices: A Review of Brian McLaren, *Finding Our Way Again: The Return of the Ancient Practices*," *The Southern Baptist Journal of Theology* 12, no.2 (Summer 2008): 62–67.

[38] *Dynamics of Spiritual Life: An Evangelical Theology of Renewal* (Downers Grove: Inter-Varsity Press, 1979) and *Renewal as a Way of Life: A Guidebook for Spiritual Growth* (Downers Grove: InterVarsity Press, 1985).

[39] These various elements are helpfully summarized in a chart on found in Lovelace, *Dynamics of Spiritual Life*, 75. For the same chart, see also *Renewal as a Way of Life*, 162.

prayer, fellowship, victory over worldliness, and the development of a theological mind.

According to Lovelace, there are two preconditions for true spirituality. Without a depth awareness of who God is and who we are in the light of that knowledge, a biblical spirituality cannot be developed. The great danger of seeking to develop a biblical spirituality in the current postmodern ambiance is being influenced by postmodernity, which is fascinated with "spiritual" talk but not at all open to a discussion of the biblical concept of sin.[40] But the central problem of humanity is sin. It is not ignorance of our true self, as Tolle and other postmodern spiritual gurus would have it, nor is it death, which is a result of sin. It is the fact that we are naturally sinners and have a deep aversion to the Holy God of the Scriptures. Before we proceed with any discussion of spirituality and spiritual disciplines, these foundational elements of knowing God and knowing humanity therefore must be in place. In the final chapter, a paradigm for developing such a foundation for a true life in the Spirit will be unpacked.

---

[40] See, for example, the way that Tolle redefines sin as to "miss the point of human existence" (*A New Earth*, 9). On the challenge of teaching about sin in the postmodern context, see Mark Dever, "Communicating Sin in a Postmodern World" in Carson, ed., *Telling the Truth*, 138–152.

13

THE SPIRIT AND KNOWING GOD THE KING[1]

Behold, our mirror is the Lord;
Open your eyes and see them in him.
And learn the manner of your face,
Then announce praises to his Spirit.
And wipe the paint from your face;
And love his holiness and put it on.

Ode of Solomon 13.1–3[2]
(*c.*120)

Knowing God and knowing man

According to Paul's words in 1 Timothy 1:5, absolutely central to Christian preaching and teaching is the development of love in the hearers and those being taught: love for God and love for one's fellow human beings. American historian Richard F. Lovelace rightly identifies such love as the main characteristic of authentic spirituality, namely, "a life which escapes from the closed circle of self-indulgence, or even self-improvement, to become absorbed in the love of God and other persons."[3] True biblical spirituality is thus first of all God-centered and then "other-centered." As we

---

[1] This chapter had its origins as a paper that was delivered at the Annual Meeting of the American Association of Christian Colleges and Seminaries, Inc., February 4, 2009. The sections on Isaiah and the Pauline epistles are taken from the author's *The God Who Draws Near: An Introduction to Biblical Spirituality* (Darlington/Webster: Evangelical Press, 2007), 13–19. Used by permission.

[2] Trans. James H. Charlesworth, *The Earliest Christian Hymnbook: The Odes of Solomon* (Eugene: Cascade Books, 2009), 39.

[3] *Renewal as a Way of Life*, 18. See also above Chapter 8.

have seen, though, self-centered spirituality is the prime characteristic of pagan culture, be it ancient or modern. In the words of Lovelace: "Self-knowledge and self-fulfillment are considered to be the core of human achievement" by pagan culture.[4] Self-knowledge is not wrong *per se*, but for it to escape ultimately from being a refined version of narcissism, it must be pursued in the light of the knowledge of God.

It is noteworthy that this is where the French theologian John Calvin begins his theological *magnum opus*, the *Institutes of the Christian Religion*, which reached its final form in 1559. True wisdom, he argues, consists of two parts: knowledge of God and self-knowledge. A true desire to know God begins with a profound dissatisfaction with ourselves. Genuine self-examination leads to an awareness of one's limits and the realization that we are dependent upon God for all that we are and have. In Calvin's words, "from the feeling of our own ignorance, vanity, poverty, infirmity, and—what is more—depravity and corruption, we recognize that the true light of wisdom, sound virtue, full abundance of every good, and purity of righteousness rest in the Lord alone."[5] But it is only when we know God that we begin to have any real knowledge of ourselves. In the 1560 French version of the *Institutes* Calvin puts it this way: "In knowing God, each of us also knows himself."[6] And in his 1559 Latin edition of the *Institutes*: "It is certain that man never achieves a clear knowledge of himself unless he has first looked upon God's face."[7] There is, thus, a

---

[4] *Renewal as a Way of Life*, 18–19.

[5] *Institutes* 1.1.1 (*Calvin: Institutes of the Christian Religion*, trans. Ford Lewis Battles and ed. John T. McNeill [The Library of Christian Classics, vol. 20; Philadelphia: The Westminster Press, 1960], 36). Subsequent references to the *Institutes* will employ this edition, but will simply identify the reference or quote by book, chapter, and section with the page number in brackets.

[6] *Calvin: Institutes of the Christian Religion*, trans. Battles and ed. McNeill, 36, n.3.

[7] *Institutes* 1.1.2, 37.

circular nature to the true knowledge of God: it is not until we know ourselves as wretched and sinful that we feel compelled to seek to know God, but it is only in the light of divine knowledge that we know what we are really like.

As Calvin develops this most basic of issues concerning human experience and discusses the human encounter with the living God of the Scriptures, it becomes clear that such an encounter is "a deeply unsettling experience."[8] Man before the majesty of God is humbled, feels himself undone, and sees something of his sinful heart's core.[9] Without such a revelation of our true nature outside of Christ, there can be no true spirituality. The first step on setting out on the spiritual journey is to know ourselves as we truly are.

The holiness of the Lord in Isaiah 6

God's holiness and justice are common themes to both the Old and New Testaments. To quote Lovelace:

> [B]oth the Old and New Testaments strongly emphasize the justice of God, his fatherly displeasure with sin in his children, and his holy anger against the rebellion and cruelty of those who are his enemies. ... Jesus' persistent warnings of divine judgment of unrepentant sinners, not merely within time but for eternity, are echoed by all the New Testament writers—even by John, the apostle of love. Although the New Covenant accents God's grace, it retains the Old Testament emphasis on his justice.[10]

---

[8] The quoted words are those of Lovelace, *Renewal as a Way of Life*, 20.

[9] *Institutes* 1.1.3. Meditate, for example, on the following Scripture texts: Isaiah 6:1–5; Habakkuk 3:1–4, 16; Luke 5:1–8; and Revelation 1:12–18.

[10] *Renewal as a Way of Life*, 24, 25–26.

One of the classical descriptions of God's holiness in the human encounter with the living God is found in Isaiah 6:1–5:

> In the year that King Uzziah died I saw the Lord sitting upon a throne, high and lifted up; and the train of his robe filled the temple. Above him stood the seraphim. Each had six wings: with two he covered his face, and with two he covered his feet, and with two he flew. And one called to another and said: "Holy, holy, holy is the Lord of hosts; the whole earth is full of his glory!" And the foundations of the thresholds shook at the voice of him who called, and the house was filled with smoke. And I said: "Woe is me! For I am lost; for I am a man of unclean lips, and I dwell in the midst of a people of unclean lips; for my eyes have seen the King, the Lord of Hosts!"[11]

In this text God is revealed as a holy God, sovereign and omnipotent over all of his creation, especially angelic and human. The effect of the revelation of God's holiness upon fallen humanity is graphically described in the way that Isaiah—God's prophet— knows himself to be above all a sinner, whose mouth, polluted as it is, well expresses the pollution of his heart.

Nothing is said about how the vision came to Isaiah, for everything is focused upon the One whom he sees: "in the year that King Uzziah died I saw the Lord." Moreover, it is noteworthy that Isaiah makes no attempt to describe what God looked like. He simply mentions that he saw the Lord "sitting upon a throne, high and lifted up; and the train of his robe filled the temple." The King of Judah may be dead, but the Lord was still sitting upon his

---

[11] ESV.

throne. This description of God as sitting upon a throne portrays him functioning as a king and sovereign.

When someone in our western world hears the word "king," any number of things might come to his mind. Fairy tales, possibly; plays of William Shakespeare (1564–1616), in which kings and queens abound; photographs of royalty gathered for the wedding of Prince Charles and Lady Diana or for Princess Diana's sad funeral. But for Isaiah and for the people of his day, the king was *the* government. The portrayal of the Lord in this manner thus emphasizes the fact that God is omnipotent, that none of his plans and purposes can fail to come to pass. The phrase that follows reinforces this portrayal of the authority of God. He is "high and exalted" over all in this universe.

But God is not only all-powerful, he is also omnipresent. There is no place in the universe that is exempt from his glorious presence. Isaiah, unable to gaze upon God's face, looks down and finds that the skirts of God's robes fill the temple in which he is standing. But not only is the temple in Jerusalem filled with the glory of God's presence, but so is the earth. As the seraphim cry out to one another: "the whole earth is full of his glory."[12]

The King of Heaven does not appear alone to the prophet, for he is surrounded by heavenly attendants, the seraphim, just as an earthly king is surrounded by the members of his court. These seraphim, of whom there is no mention elsewhere in the Old Testament, are clearly an order of angelic beings who minister to the Lord with unceasing praise and service. Yet even these heavenly beings dare not look upon the face of their Creator; but in reverent awe and humility they shield their faces and feet. Isaiah sees them

---

[12] Isaiah 6:2. In Psalm 19:1 this thought is taken one step further: "The heavens declare the glory of God, and the sky above proclaims his handiwork" (ESV). The God with whom we have to deal is an all-powerful King, whose glory fills the entirety of his universe!

standing above the throne of their Lord, ever ready to obey his commands. He hears them proclaiming one to another, in a mighty fugue, the holiness of their Creator: "Holy, holy, holy is the Lord of hosts; the whole earth is full of his glory!"[13] These seraphim are well aware that there is only One who is worthy of their adoration and praise, for he alone is intrinsically holy.

To call God "holy" is first of all to speak of his transcendence over the entire created realm and to affirm his total independence of his creation, which could not exist for a second without him. In the words of Richard Lovelace: "God's holiness is his differentness, for the word *holy* means 'separate or distinct.' God is different from all created beings."[14] Then, in a derivative meaning, his holiness speaks of his moral purity, as Isaiah 6:5 goes on to imply.

The effect of this vision upon Isaiah is devastating and traumatic: "Woe is me! For I am lost; for I am a man of unclean lips, and I dwell in the midst of a people of unclean lips; for my eyes have seen the King, the Lord of Hosts!"[15] It is only on the basis of a proper view of God, that man can attain a true estimation of himself. Now that Isaiah has seen the authority and majesty of the Lord, he sees himself as he really is—as all human beings actually are. He is a man whose sinful heart has polluted his lips and so prevented him from joining the song of the seraphim, as they praise their Lord with lips that are pure and stainless and free from sin. And if he cannot join in the praise of the seraphim, how much more are his polluted lips unfit to speak for God!

As the vision of Isaiah 6 unfolds, God reveals himself also as God of mercy, for he goes on to cleanse the prophet with a

---

[13] Isaiah 6:3 ESV.
[14] *Renewal as a Way of Life*, 21.
[15] Isaiah 6:5 ESV.

"burning coal" from the altar in Jerusalem.[16] But before there is this good news of "cleansing," there is the distressing revelation of being found a sinner in the presence of a holy God.

Knowing the depth of human sin

One important set of biblical texts that deal with human sinfulness in believers are the letters of the Apostle Paul. In the providence of God, one of the reasons for their being in the canon of Scripture is to provide Christian theology with clear teaching on the nature of the human condition and its consequent need of salvation.

One of the key terms that Paul uses to describe human sinfulness is the "flesh" (*sarx*). The usage of this term varies throughout Paul's writings. In 1 Corinthians 15:39 it is used to describe either the physical flesh as distinct from the skeletal structure or possibly it is being used as a synonym for the whole body. In Romans 1:3 it is nothing less than the entirety of physical existence. Galatians 1:16 uses the word to mean "human beings." But Paul normally uses the word *sarx* with a profoundly negative connotation. When he uses it thus, it stands for the whole human personality—body, soul, mind and emotions—as it functions in independent self-sufficiency, apart from God and the control of his Holy Spirit.[17] A good example of this latter usage is Galatians 5:16–18, where the Apostle lists the "works of the flesh."

What does the "flesh" entail when it has this more negative coloring? It is that in the human person which is utterly and irrevocably opposed to the Spirit of God. The flesh is oriented mightily towards self. As Lovelace remarks:

---

[16] Isaiah 6:6.

[17] Lovelace *Renewal as a Way of Life*, 72; Anthony Thistleton, "Flesh," in Colin Brown, ed., *The New International Dictionary of New Testament Theology* (Grand Rapids: Zondervan, 1975), I, 680.

> The flesh is deeply *self-centered*. Ultimately it looks at all issues from a selfish perspective. "What's in it for me?" is the question it invariably asks. It produces many ingenious compounds: self-confidence, self- consciousness, self-importance, self-indulgence, self-pity, self-righteousness, self-satisfaction, self-fulfillment.[18]

A state of war thus marks the relationship between the flesh and the Holy Spirit. It is a war in which there is no neutral ground. Look at what flesh seeks to encourage: "sexual immorality, impurity, sensuality, idolatry, sorcery, enmity, strife, jealousy, fits of anger, rivalries, dissensions, divisions, envy, drunkenness, orgies."[19] How radically different is the path on which Spirit is directing the believer: "the fruit of the Spirit is love, joy, peace, patience, kindness, goodness, faithfulness, gentleness, self-control."[20] The result of this conflict, as deadly as any war fought on this planet, is that one cannot do what one wants to do. Unless defeated by a greater power, the sin within our human frame will keep us from doing the good we desire.[21] The central solution that Paul gives us is the presence and power of the Spirit. Thus, he writes: "walk by the Spirit, and you will not gratify the desires of the flesh."[22] This conflict is so intense, that unless one wholly leans on the Spirit, sin will triumph. And the Spirit, true to his Christocentric bent, points men and women to the unique sacrifice of the Son at the cross as *the* supreme place of cleansing from the pollution of sin and *the* strong resource in the face of sin's power. As the Puritan divine John Owen rightly says: "There is

---

[18] Lovelace, *Renewal as a Way of Life*, 79.
[19] Galatians 5:19–21 ESV.
[20] Galatians 5:22–23 ESV.
[21] Galatians 5:17.
[22] Galatians 5:16 ESV.

no death of sin without the death of Christ. ... The Spirit alone brings the cross of Christ into our hearts with its sin-killing power; for by the Spirit we are baptized into the death of Christ."[23]

A balanced perspective

In the history of the Church some Christians have regarded this conflict as result of a lack of faith or spirituality. The Wesleyan/Holiness tradition is particularly prone to this perspective. Building upon the theological perspectives of John Wesley (1703–1791) and his lieutenant John Fletcher (1729–1785), many Christians in the nineteenth-century Holiness movement "believed that it was possible for believers to live a perfect life without sin. They were able to believe this because they had redefined sin as conscious willful acts of disobedience to known laws."[24]

But the truth of the matter is quite different. Those who claim to have attained sinless perfection have simply not come to grips with the fact that the whole of our being is permeated with the poison of sin. Kenneth Prior employs an apt example to illustrate the human condition: "Sin is like a drop of ink in a glass of water. It is diffused throughout the glass. The water may be only slightly blue, but nonetheless the entire contents of the glass are colored to some degree."[25] Sin, as the transgression of God's law, produces in man a twofold need: freedom from the guilt of sin and cleansing from its defilement. The first need has been met through the death of Christ, by which we are justified,[26] while the second need is satisfied by the work of sanctification. The believer

---

[23] *Of the Mortification of Sin in Believers* in *The Works of John Owen* (1850–1853 ed.; repr. Edinburgh/Carlisle: The Banner of Truth Trust, 1967), VI, 33, 86.

[24] *Renewal as a Way of Life*, 73–74.

[25] Kenneth Prior, *The Way of Holiness. A Study in Christian Growth* (Rev. ed.; Downers Grove: InterVarsity Press, 1982), 37.

[26] Romans 5:1; 8:1–2.

has been delivered from being under the tyranny of sin and being sin's slave.[27] Yet, sin's presence has not been eradicated from the believer's life. Sin may have lost its dominion, but it can still bring shame, spiritual defeat, and confusion into the life of a Christian.

Scottish theologian Sinclair Ferguson uses the imagery of addiction to describe this ongoing struggle with the flesh and sin. "Although I have been delivered from addiction to sin, its presence remains. I experience withdrawal symptoms and remain weakened by its devastating impact on my life."[28] And, as Ferguson further notes, rather than the empowering presence of Spirit in the believer's life bringing deliverance from this spiritual warfare, "it is the presence of the Spirit that produces these conflicts."[29] Sanctification is a progressive work, an ongoing process that is begun at regeneration but is never completed in this life.

Having said all this, we must remember that the keynote of the Christian life in the Spirit as the New Testament conceives it is not the struggle against sin. Rather, as Lovelace puts it: "Walking with God is essentially a positive thing. The Bible does not point us toward constant introspection. Instead, it helps us to focus on the privileges of being in Christ and enjoying fellowship with God."[30] And this is why joy is so often linked to the Spirit in the New Testament and why Paul can define the ambience in the Empire of Christ as consisting of "righteousness and peace and joy in the Holy Spirit."[31]

---

[27] See Romans 6:17–22.

[28] Sinclair B. Ferguson, "The Reformed View" in Donald L. Alexander, ed., *Christian Spirituality: Five Views of Sanctification* (Downers Grove: InterVarsity Press, 1988), 62.

[29] Ferguson, "Reformed View," 63.

[30] *Renewal as a Way of Life*, 78–79.

[31] Romans 14:17. On joy and the Spirit, see also, Luke 10:21; Galatians 5:22; 1 Thessalonians 1:6.

14

A CONCLUDING WORD

"We bow ... before the Holy Spirit"

Gregory of Nyssa
(*c.*335–*c.*395)

This book is dedicated to the memory of my mother, Teresa Veronica Haykin, née O'Gorman (1933–1976), who died on March 9, 1976, a few months after she was born again by the Spirit of God in the fall of 1975. At the time of her going to be with the Lord, I was nearing the end of the second year of my Master of Religion program at Wycliffe College, the University of Toronto. The previous fall I had written my first paper in Patristics, on Novatian's *On the Trinity*. God gave me a love for the Fathers through that first encounter, and so it was, in the weeks after my mother's death I decided to write a paper on Irenaeus' concept of the beatific vision for a course being taught by Eugene R. Fairweather (1921–2002), then of Trinity College. Prof. Fairweather was a remarkable man, a polymath in many ways, and a delight to listen to as a lecturer. He had distinct eccentricities, though, one of which was a habit of not returning students' papers and even occasionally not submitting marks for the students in his courses! Happily, though, he returned my paper on Irenaeus and gave me a mark on it that was duly submitted to the Registrar at my home college, Wycliffe College. He wrote at the close of my paper that he hoped I would continue on in Patristics, an encouragement that no doubt helped a little to determine the direction of my future scholarly

189

path. But what mattered most to me at the time was the way that Irenaeus' biblical view of the future was such a comfort to me following the death of my mother.

Central to Irenaeus' eschatological vision is the fact that the Holy Spirit is "the ladder of ascent to God."[1] The Holy Spirit enables the redeemed to ascend to the vision of God by first "preparing humanity in the Son of God, the Son then leads humanity to the Father, and the Father bestows incorruption for eternal life, which comes to each one as a result of seeing God. Just as those who see the light are in the light and share in its splendor, so are those who see God: they are in God and share in his splendor. The splendor gives them life; and thus those who see God lay hold of life."[2] The division between Creator and creature is not violated, but men and women finally realize the purpose of their creation: to glory in God and indeed to be so filled with that glory they become brilliant reflections of it.[3] This is life indeed.

It was a message I sorely needed to hear in the midst of experiencing my mother's death. And it is a message that I still need to hear and rejoice in: to be indwelt by the Spirit of God is to have life—a life of love and joy and hope. And it is one that I need to share with family and friends and in the public square.

---

[1] *Against the Heresies* 3.24.1, trans. J. Patout Burns and Gerald M. Fagin, *The Holy Spirit* (Message of the Fathers of the Church, vol. 3; Wilmington: Michael Glazier, Inc., 1984), 36.

[2] *Against the Heresies* 4.20.5–6, trans. Michael A.G. Haykin.

[3] See the similar reflections on this by Basil of Caesarea, *On the Holy Spirit* 9.23 and Jonathan Edwards, *Religious Affections*, ed. John E. Smith (The Works of Jonathan Edwards, vol. 2; New Haven: Yale University Press, 1959), 200–201. A portion of Edwards' reflection is cited above, page 31. I am thankful to Dr. Adam McClendon, who was one of my doctoral students at The Southern Baptist Theological Seminary, and who drew my attention to the text by Edwards. I immediately saw its similarity to that of Basil.

The Spirit and the Bride say, "Come."

Revelation 22:17 ESV.

READING ABOUT THE HOLY SPIRIT

Up until the 1960s and 1970s, it was a commonplace in the publishing world of Evangelicalism that there was very little of substance written on the person and work of the Holy Spirit. If this statement were being made about the twentieth century to that point in time, it is, with the exception of Pentecostal authors, broadly correct. But left to stand as an absolute statement with no qualification, it is quite wrong.

First of all, there is, of course, the Patristic literature on the Spirit, of which key texts have been helpfully collected in J. Patout Burns and Gerald M. Fagin, *The Holy Spirit* (1984)[1] and now Joel C. Elowsky, ed., *We Believe in the Holy Spirit* (2009).[2] If I were to name individual texts from the Fathers on the Spirit that have been influential on my thinking I would note especially, in the second and third centuries, *The Odes of Solomon*,[3] Irenaeus' *Against Heresies*,[4] and Cyprian's *Letter to Donatus*[5] and in the fourth

---

[1] *The Holy Spirit* (Message of the Fathers of the Church, vol. 3; Wilmington: Michael Glazier, Inc., 1984).

[2] *We Believe in the Holy Spirit* (Ancient Christian Doctrine, vol. 4; Downers Grove: InterVarsity Press, 2009).

[3] See the translation of this gem by James H. Charlesworth, *The Earliest Christian Hymnbook: The Odes of Solomon* (Eugene: Cascade Books, 2009).

[4] It is amazing that there is no contemporary translation of this work available in English. There are portions here and there, but nothing since the Victorian translation reproduced often in *The Ante-Nicene Fathers* by Alexander Roberts and W.H. Rambaut in A. Cleveland Coxe, arr., *The Apostolic Fathers with Justin Martyr and Irenaeus* (Ante-Nicene Fathers, vol. 1; 1885 ed.; repr. New York: Charles Scribner's Sons, 1903), 315–567.

[5] Cyprian, *To Donatus*, trans. Roy J. Deferrari, *Saint Cyprian: Treatises* (New York: Fathers of the Church, Inc., 1958), 5–21.

century, Athanasius' *Letters to Serapion*,[6] Hilary's work on the Trinity[7]—which is a very fine study, but completely overshadowed by Augustine's work with the same title—Basil of Caesarea's *On the Holy Spirit*,[8] and Macarius-Symeon's homilies.[9] Augustine' *Confessions* has also been central in my thinking about the sort of spirituality that the Spirit nurtures.[10]

Of the works by the Reformers and Puritans, John Calvin's *Institutes* has been quite influential,[11] as have John Owen's massive study of the Spirit,[12] John Bunyan's *I Will Pray With the Spirit*,[13] and John Howe's series of sermons on the outpouring of the Spirit.[14] I found a helpful guide to Puritan pneumatology in Geoffrey F. Nuttall's superb *The Holy Spirit in Puritan Faith and Experience* (2nd ed.; 1947).[15] In the eighteenth century, among the notable works that have shaped my thinking about the Holy Spirit have been Charles Wesley's hymns, George Whitefield's sermons,[16] and, above all, the writings of the theologian of revival,

---

[6] C.R.B. Shapland, *The Letters of Saint Athanasius Concerning the Holy Spirit* (London: Epworth Press, 1951).

[7] *Saint Hilary of Poitiers: The Trinity*, trans. Stephen McKenna (New York: Fathers of the Church, Inc., 1954).

[8] Basil of Caesarea, *On the Holy Spirit*, trans. David Anderson (Crestwood, New York: St Vladimir's Seminary Press, 1980).

[9] *Pseudo-Macarius: The Fifity Spiritual Homilies and The Great Letter*, trans. and ed. George A. Maloney (New York/Mahwah: Paulist Press, 1992).

[10] There are numerous translations of this spiritual classic.

[11] *Calvin: Institutes of the Christian Religion*, trans. Ford Lewis Battles and ed. John T. McNeill (The Library of Christian Classics, vols. 20–21; Philadelphia: The Westminster Press, 1960), 2 vols.

[12] *The Works of John Owen*, ed. William H. Goold (1850–1853 ed.; repr. Edinburgh: The Banner of Truth Trust, 1965), vol. III and IV.

[13] *John Bunyan: The Doctrine of the Law and Grace unfolded and I will pray with the Spirit*, ed. Richard L. Greaves (Oxford: Clarendon Press, 1976).

[14] *The Prosperous State of the Christian Interest Before the End of Time, by A Plentiful Effusion of the Holy Spirit; Considered in Fifteen Sermons, on Ezek. 39:29* in *The Works of the Rev. John Howe, M.A.* (London: Frederick Westley and A.H. Davis, 1832). This series is quite rare, and the author hopes to bring to press shortly an edition of these sermons.

[15] *The Holy Spirit in Puritan Faith and Experience* (2nd ed.; Oxford: Basil Blackwell, 1947).

[16] *Sermons on Important Subjects* (London: Thomas Tegg, 1833), *passim*.

Jonathan Edwards, especially his *Religious Affections*, that lays out the nature of true piety.[17] I also need to mention that a turning-point in my own scholarly interests came as a result of reading Andrew Fuller's *The Promise of the Spirit, the grand encouragement in promoting the Gospel* (1812), a great tract on relying on the Spirit to fulfil the Great Commission.[18]

Of modern works that have been extremely helpful in my thinking about and experience of the Spirit—and now the situation is quite the reverse of what prevailed among Evangelicals for the first two-thirds of the twentieth century, there is so much written on the Spirit—there is Richard Lovelace's *Dynamics of Spiritual Life: An Evangelical Theology of Renewal* (1979),[19] J.I. Packer's *Keep In Step With The Spirit* (1984)[20] and a variety of smaller pieces by Packer on the Spirit, Sinclair B. Ferguson's *The Holy Spirit* (1996)[21] along with D. Martyn Lloyd-Jones' teaching on the work of the Holy Spirit, which stirred up no small controversy, in his *Joy Unspeakable* (1985) and *The Sovereign Spirit. Discerning His Gifts* (1985).[22] Though I cannot say I fully endorse all of Lloyd-Jones' views, his desire to know the biblical experience of the Spirit and not veer off into an Evangelical hyper-rationalism or hyper-intellectualism is highly commendable. His prayerful expectation for the Spirit and

---

[17] *Religious Affections*, ed. John E. Smith (*The Works of Jonathan Edwards*, vol. 2; New Haven: Yale University Press, 1959).

[18] *The Complete Works of the Rev. Andrew Fuller*, revised Joseph Belcher (1845 ed.; repr. Harrisonburg: Sprinkle Publications, 1988), III, 359–363.

[19] *Dynamics of Spiritual Life: An Evangelical Theology of Renewal* (Downers Grove: InterVarsity Press, 1979).

[20] J.I. Packer, *Keep In Step With The Spirit* (Old Tappan: Fleming H. Revell Co., 1984). A second edition of this work is now available.

[21] Sinclair B. Ferguson, *The Holy Spirit* (Downers Grove: InterVarsity Press, 1996).

[22] *Joy Unspeakable* (Wheaton: Harold Shaw Publishers, 1985) and *The Sovereign Spirit. Discerning His Gifts* (Wheaton: Harold Shaw Publishers, 1985). The first of these volumes was published in North America as *The Baptism and Gifts of the Spirit* (Grand Rapids: Baker Book House, 1996).

his transforming presence has been a model for my own life and prayers.

About the Author

Michael A.G. Haykin, FRHistS, was born in England of Irish and Kurdish parents. He serves as Chair and Professor of Church History at the Southern Baptist Theological Seminary, Louisville, Kentucky and is the Director of The Andrew Fuller Center for Baptist Studies, also at Southern. Haykin has a B.A in Philosophy from the University of Toronto (1974), a Master of Religion from Wycliffe College, the University of Toronto (1977), and a Doctorate of Theology in Church History from Wycliffe College and University of Toronto (1982). He also serves as Professor of Church History at Heritage Theological Seminary, Cambridge, Ontario. He and his wife Alison have their home in Dundas, Ontario.

Scripture Index

Date Read	Name

Made in the USA
Monee, IL
07 July 2026